THE BLACK TRUTH
Behind
White Lies

By
David Lee the
Author

THE BLACK TRUTH BEHIND WHITE LIES
Copyright © 2016 by DAVID LEE

ISBN -13:978-0-578-18157-8

Printed in the USA by 48HrBooks
(www.48HrBooks.com)

About the Author

David Lee has been a victim of racial abuse through verbal, mental and physical terrorism with no necessary means of retaliation. After three encounters with the Indiana Department of Corrections, David Lee is sharing his experience and knowledge that is only a reflection of the pain that he's experienced while being a black man in America.

While incarcerated, David read many books of different philosophers and discovered many inconsistencies. Be prepared to be educated, enlightened and somewhat entertained while exploring science, politics, history, religion, economics and racism through the eyes of David Lee.

David Lee is an explorer of scientific, political, historical, economic and biblical knowledge. He will use many Bible scriptures that will decipher the many falsehoods that are being taught by many Christians and non-Christians alike.

It would be wise to have a Bible, dictionary or a digital device near so you can uncover the truth with David Lee. Be prepared to have your 3rd eye opened.

www.davidleetheauthor.com
davidleetheauthor@gmail.com

Preface

The world is in danger because of the corruption of white lies. Violence and death have covered America like a gray storm cloud and it has become totally out of control. We are beginning to mirror the times of the civil rights movement which means that the world needs to be reformed, rearranged and reconstructed once again.

Instead of an urban fictional novel, I decided to write a book filled with substance. Something that would help bring knowledge to the lost souls and inquiring minds of our society.

All of my life experiences have led to the content in this book. I hope my interpretation of the many topics brings light to those who are blind.

I would like to thank God for giving me the strength, desire, knowledge, and courage to write this book revealing the Black Truth behind white lies.

David Lee the Author

Table of Contents

PART I The White man System 8

   Alcohol Drugs and Doctors 11

   The Declaration of Independence 16

   American Flag 18

   Nazi / Swastika 19

   American Terrorism 21

PART II Fake Economic System 26

   Two Faced Politician 26

   Understanding the Fake American Dream 28

   Fake Money 30

   Fake Job 32

   Fake Name 35

   Compare the Economic Tornado to the Movie 'The Wizard of Oz' 36

PART III Science Knowledge & Colors 45

   Unveil Their Secrets 45

   Black 47

   White 49

   Red White and Blue 51

   Humans 53

PART IV Angels, Aliens, Demons 56

   Michael vs. Lucifer 56

   The Reptile 60

   White Devil Domination 64

Aliens..66

PART V Powers of the Air vs Family Life.....................70

The Apple=Computer 666....................................70

Cartoons..76

Fake Reality TV...77

Music..78

PART VI Two Broken Covenants.............................84

PART VII Black Truth about Christianity...................89

1 The Trinity...92

2 JESUS IS God...93

3 CALLING man FATHER...................................94

4 Resurrection Day..94

5 The New Law..95

6 JOHN 3:16...96

7 THE SABBATH DAY..97

White Jesus...104

PART VIII Intelligent Designer..............................108

The Austral –Hetero-Homo Formula..................110

Evolution, School, and the Outcome...................112

The first seven Jim Crow Laws...........................116

The second 7 Jim Crow Laws.............................116

PART VIIII World's Biggest Gangs...........................117

The Criminal System..117

Citizen Vs Felon..119

The Police..121

CIA...126

True Freemasons.................................128

Illuminati, 911 and the Media............133

13 Most Powerful States 142

All American Terrorist 145

PART X Movement to One Nation 149

The Message 149

The Originators 154

1 Nation..158

African American Flag........................162

Your Life Matters 164

Skits 166

Trading Places 166

The American Party 169

Works Cited 173

Dedication..176

PART I The White man System

The Black Truth came in the beginning. When darkness covered the face of the deep, the Creator sent a bright light. This light penetrated the darkness and released itself from the gravitational pull of the manifestation of blackness. The light is faster than the speed of light, and it connects the quantum strings of life that connect to everything. The light is consciousness, wisdom, life, energy and love. The light is eternal and infinitive. The light is God. The light is the Black Truth. A white lie came after the Creator sent the light. The white lie is the devil.

A white lie is used to misrepresent the truth. Since this type of lie is a half-truth, it is taught by the white man as being polite and harmless. It is accepted to be a lie that is good. How can a white lie or any lie be good? The power of the white lie has influenced the entire earth's population in some form or fashion. Almost true or half true is still a lie America! The devil is the father of lies so the devil must also be white and a misrepresentation of the truth just like a white lie.

The European nations call themselves white, and some of them are considered the elites of America. These people influence the entire world with white lies. They are the number of man, 666 and their white lies help create white laws meant to oppress non-whites and lower class whites.

The European American nation invented the white lie so there will always be almost true laws enforced. The European elites have always enforced all of the white lies known as laws, upon the backs of African Americans. The European nation calls the African American nation black. They use to call them niggers, they still do by saying the N-word in place of nigger. It is the same concept of a white lie. So saying n-word is a polite and harmless way of saying nigger. The extremely racists Europeans who have told white lies hated the African American nation and made plans to kill African Americans hundreds of years ago. The white lies have corrupted the minds of many white and black Americans. It's time that the Black Truth be revealed.

A white lie feels good to most people even though it is wrong. One lie brings another lie. Most people smile when they tell a white lie so that their face looks convincing while they're lying. The devil is the chief deceiver, and he hides behind rich and powerful men's smile. The lie is white and the white devil telling the lie can be a white man, black man or any man. The white lie makes a situation seem right, but it's wrong. When the white lie is revealed, the Black Truth is brought out in the open for everyone to see.

The white lie that made you smile has turned your smile into a frown. The Black Truth shatters the belief in the white lie. The repercussions from revealing the Black truth behind the white lie have led many good people to commit violent acts. These acts have led many to prison or the cemetery.

The truth can set you free, incarcerate you or have you killed. Is it better to not tell the white lie and stay clear of the inevitable pain the white lie will bring? The white man teaches us to tell white lies but never reveals the consequences of the action from the lie. True freedom begins when you release yourself from the negative influences of the white devils. This would free many from vices and build the ability to break free from mental, physical and chemical chains. It's time to take handcuffs off and the threat of prison. It's time to wake up and fight the white devils and take our kingdom back.

This book will prove that a white lie is a lie, and there is no way it could ever be good. God is the personification of Good. He is a super immortal being, a positive conscious force of life bringing truth, peace, and love to all men and women. God is the life-giver, and He does not give us a spirit of fear but power, love and a sound mind. After reading this book you will know that the white lies of the white man system is not of God, it is of the devil.

> D- Devious
> E- Evil
> V-Vindictive
> I- Insane
> L-Luciferian
> S-Serpents

The devil is the personification of evil, and he is a deceitful, lying, manipulating, murdering, immortal super being who can operate in our world and in the world that is unseen. The devil is not a good guy. He is the destroyer and liar who wants to bring white lies, war and death to all men and women, especially black men and women. He is the chief hate crime criminal and terrorist who wants to drop atomic bombs on you and bring worldwide destruction. He is the life taker. 2 Corinthians 4:4 "In whom the god of this world hath blinded the minds of them which believe not lest the light of the glorious gospel of Christ who is the image of God should shine on them. Those who totally trust in this worldly god are being deceived."

This worldly god is the white man. Read the book of Job and you will understand that the white man and the devil are the same people. The earth was given to them, they travel inside and outside of the world, they are always looking for good people to kill, they make people kill people and animals, they make bombs and lightning fall from the sky to kill people and animals, they steal from people and kill more people, they mess with the weather and it kills people, finally they make diseases which have caused quadrillions to die throughout many centuries.

When you think about these evil things and compare them to your knowledge of the laws and origin of the American nation, you will understand that most laws that you obey come from a twisted, ungodly and racist arrangement of ordinances created by the white man. The white man is god on this blue planet, and they are the leaders who make the laws. You are encouraged to trust in them but Psalm 146:3 says "Don't put your trust in human leaders. Don't believe in people that can't save you 4 when they die; they return to the ground."

Alcohol Drugs and Doctors

Let us analyze and discuss these two ordinances that are in the body of the white man system pertaining to alcohol and drugs. Prohibition was meant to eradicate the temptation of liquor it had the unintended effect of turning many law-abiding citizens into criminals. Alcohol was considered evil and detrimental to your health and the main contributor to the downfall of being able to achieve and maintain the American and Christian family way of life. The end of Prohibition and the empowerment of the white man made it lawful for you to drink alcohol. It is still one of the chief causes of murders, crime and domestic violence around the world. The all-knowing white man has proclaimed that drinking alcohol is okay so everyone drinks. The law has allowed a liquor store to be built on almost every corner in every urban and inner city neighborhood.

The creators of the law appear to want a lot of inner city non-white families to be eradicated by liquor consumption and the destruction it may cause. Why drink? What do these communities have other than liquor stores for the youth and families? There are a lot of churches and parks in inner-city neighborhoods but for some reason they're not too far from the liquor stores which are sometimes right across the street! High off the Lord then get drunk. As theoretical physicist, Jim Gates would say, "This is weird."

Recreation centers are being closed, and after school programs are so expensive, the residents in the communities cannot afford to send their children. Big corporations target inner city youth with alcohol campaigns featuring entertainment figures in commercials using catchy popular music in their radio advertising. Sending out the subliminal message to buy, drink, get drunk, be cool like your favorite entertainer and turn down for what.

The white man is very smart and conniving. The white man orchestrated this manipulating marketing scheme to destroy all inner city neighborhoods by keeping them drunk and not focused on the tragic state of black America. This subliminal messaging is now under attack because it is affecting white mainstream American youth, as seen in their movie and music idols who have extreme addictions and increasing suicide rates.

A liquor license has now become one of the most sought after licenses in America. It is also one of the most expensive and hardest to obtain. The white man knows that the holder of this license has the power to destroy families and entire communities. The liquor license holder can also reestablish responsibility in alcohol use in the inner city communities.

Unfortunately, the white lies and power felt amongst these license holders prohibits most of them from saving their communities. People don't understand that alcohol is a drug. You can get extremely addicted to it and turn into an unstable, crazy, funky breath drunk person. Alcohol has caused more deaths than cocaine and heroin put together. The white man created alcohol laws, and they made this drug legal at 21. Since this drug became legal, Christian folk can get a little high too.

Tobacco is another drug that millions of people will swear it's not. Some tobacco smokers will even criticize marijuana smokers even though they both do the same thing, smoke! The white man says you can smoke cigarettes at age 18, so it makes it ok to do this drug because the white man said so. This drug causes more addictions and deaths than cocaine, heroin, and alcohol put together, but who cares about statistics.

Marijuana is semi-illegal and has been prescribed legally by doctors for years. My question is, if tobacco kills and marijuana heals, why hasn't tobacco been illegal all this time and marijuana legal? There was a time during the 17 and 1800's when it was legal in America and farmers were forced by law, to grow hemp. Marijuana proved to provide healing until the Federal Marijuana Tax Act of 1937 and the demonizing scare tactics of Harry Anslinger and Jay Edgar Hoover during the 1960's. It became labeled as illegal and punishable by jail time.

The laws were changed so that the white system can make trillions through the criminal justice system while in other countries it's been legal since the 70's. Ronald and Nancy Reagan told us to say no to drugs, and if we're caught doing them, we're looked at as criminals whether it's for medicinal purposes or not. The white system doesn't openly tell you that all drugs are tested by doing experiments on military soldiers, animals, and other people to see the chemical reaction. After this process, it's then determined how the drug will be distributed and marketed. The white man still has population control and marketing ideas in these chemical projects that started long ago.

Marijuana, the so-called gateway drug leads to the community destroyer drugs cocaine, crack, heroine, and meth. In the past, the white man made cocaine legal, and it was once used as a remedy for illnesses. Coca-Cola was introduced in the 1800s as a medicinal potion and contained doses of the incredibly addictive drug cocaine. The white system legalizes drug dealing, and the legal drug dealers prescribe pills that have caused more people to become addicted or die than all illegal drugs put together. The legal drug dealers are called doctors, and your pass to purchase is known as a prescription.

Street doctors are no different from legitimate doctors. They both prescribe chemicals that get people relaxed, sleepy, high, addicted and dead. They both get high on their own supply. They both make a lot of money. The violence and threat of prison street doctor's face will hardly ever reach white collar doctors. They are incorporated so very seldom do they go to jail for controlled buys or when one of their patients overdoses.

It's all a drug money making conspiracy because scientists and chemists run the drug world, and they are the ones who came up with the formula of baking soda mix to make crack cocaine. The penalties for illegal drug dealing is higher for drugs that are white compared to the drug that is green because the influence and addiction is extremely higher and the dealers make enormous amounts of untaxed money, white money.

The white system hates the black man making white money, which is why white dope charges and the three strike laws were created to end the black man's American dream of being a cocaine cowboy. It doesn't matter, whatever the white system says is the law. They could make cocaine legal again and just like that it would be in stores next to the cigarettes.

How do you think drugs get into the country in the first place?

The white system influences the military, and they are brothers of the CIA, Homeland Security, and other Authorities. They have satellite radars and cameras in and outside of the atmosphere, so they know what's going on. It's just the black man is the poster child for drug dealing while the white man uses his military police power to let metric tons of drugs come in the country on planes, trains, trucks, boats, and submarines.

You may have watched white Americas' version of the American Gangster. One of the truths in the movie is street drug dealers don't own the boats and planes bringing drugs to America. The owners are the corporate drug dealers, and the military is in on all deals.

The white system now says it's ok for same-sex marriage to be legal so now the white man is rearranging the laws of nature. America is forced to fall in with whatever the white man says. The white man has influenced every document and it has brainwashed people into believing in white lies as if they were truth. Let us examine some of their documents and banners of untruth and dishonor.

The Declaration of Independence

'We hold these truths to be self-evident that all men are created equal, and they are endowed by their Creator with certain unalienable rights and among these are life liberty and the pursuit of happiness.'

This is the most famous white lie in the Declaration of Independence! If this is considered to be a statement of truth, then the whole assembly of the United States is in violation and full of untruths.

The Declaration of Independence does not have anything to do with non-rich white America or non-European America. The founding fathers were in violation of this declaration because all men were not free in 1776. As a matter of fact, several members of the cabinet still owned slaves when they were supposedly liberated from Great Britain. The white man conquerors came to the new world America and took the Indian's land while raping and killing thousands of them. The white man gave them diseases which caused millions of them to die. The white man has nerve to create the oxymoron

Thanksgiving. I don't think the Indians were thankful after the Indian Removal Act of 1830. The Trail of Tears forced thousands of sick, crying and dying Indians to leave their land on foot. They even forced and bribed some of the Indians to join them to fight against their brothers and sisters. Millions of acres of land were stolen from the Indians along with natural resources. Before the American Indian conquest was the African conquest, when the white man traveled to Africa to trade, trick, deceive and steal a whole nation.

The white man detained thousands of Africans bringing them to America forcing them to be slaves and work the lands that they took from the Indians. Millions of Africans perished from this process. The white man conquered, colonized, dehumanized and eventually integrated both the Indians and Africans into somewhat of an English European clone society. More African and Indian people were enslaved and murdered during the white American conquest than all the wars in history. The white man performed generational genocide to create a systematical illusion of independence. These acts were committed all in the name of Jesus.

There was so much evil done by these white supremacist that were called holy Christians. Their white God and their white Jesus was preached and accepted by force. The same time that they were teaching these white Jesus gospels they were killing, stealing and destroying the Indian-Mexican and African nations. These acts became justifiable by their laws. These are the same acts of the devil in John 10:10, proving that the Declaration of Independence is a white lie because the truth is evident, that they believe that all white men are created equal and the only unalienable rights given to non-white men, are death, slavery and the pursuit of sadness. It's time to wake up.

American Flag

With the American citizens entrusted to freedom and loyalty, the American flag became the banner of truth, justice and honor. In the past, students paid homage to the American flag by reciting the Pledge of Allegiance. I have discovered serious conflicts with this pledge. Between 1924 and 1954 the Pledge of Allegiance was worded:

> *"I pledge allegiance to the flag of the United States of America and to the Republic for which it stands; one nation indivisible with liberty and justice for all."*

In 1954 during the McCarthy era and communism scare, Congress passed a bill which was signed to add the words "under God."

> *"I pledge allegiance to the flag of the United States of America and to the Republic for which it stands; one nation under God indivisible with liberty and justice for all.*

Paying homage to the flag was supposed to stand for something that was true. A nation that has the blessing of the one almighty God. Even after removing under

God the pledge is still an untruth. Since when has America been indivisible with liberty and justice for all? America was built on being divisive by race, class, social standing and sex since the beginning. European communities have always been capitalist, commoners and those of upper class.

Who decided these families were of nobility and others were not? It was just accepted as such and has been from the beginning. Open a newspaper, turn on the news and tell me if you see justice for an entire society. How can a country that preaches to be indivisible with liberty and justice for all, break every commandment and enslave so many people?

Freedom is not free; billions have paid for freedom through death. America has taken God out of everything that makes society a just society. The world only turns to God in times of turmoil. The first statement in times of harm is 'God bless America'.

Why should God bless America?

Why has America taken God out of everything American?

The Pledge of Allegiance is in Violation and is full of white lies.

Nazi / Swastika

The Confederate and the Nazi flags are the banners of racist white American history. The Nazi swastika currently stands for white power and the empowerment of the Aryan nation. It became the symbol for the German Nazis in the 1930's. Did you know thousands of years ago the swastika belonged to the Asian Indian Aryans? Their religion was Hinduism, and they worshiped multiple gods. They practiced peace, meditation, and selflessness.

Hitler adopted Their flag because of a similar white power hostile takeover. The light skin Aryans invaded the darker skin Aryans the same way Hitler did the Jews. That turned the flag that once stood for peace into European pride, white power, class division, war, and conquering. The total hatred toward the Jews created hate crimes of terror. Millions of Jews perished under the command of the great white devil Adolph Hitler. The Nazi swastika is the flag of hate; after hate comes hate crimes. This flag is still being promoted today by white supremacists in the United States of America.

The passion of racism and hate in the Nazi flag is the same passion that is in the flag that stands for the Confederate States of America, which also displays a criss-cross form. In fact, the Confederate flag is related to the Nazi Swastika because both flags now represent the same white pride and passion to perform genocide of an entire race. The African Indian people were the target for terror by the Confederate White Europeans, just like the Jews were the target for terror by the German Europeans.

The Confederate flag has 13 stars which stand for the 13 southern colonies. You will find in this book that the number 13 connects to the entire white man system of power. The Confederate flag was the banner of honor of the Confederate army, and their general was named Robert E. Lee. They fought for white southern pride and stood for the white citizens of The Confederate States of America.

This flag was adopted by the all-American terrorist group the KKK. They are a terrorist group that calls themselves Christians. In the past, this Christian terrorist group had connections to get away with burning crosses in yards and murdering black people. Currently, this white American group terrorizes all ethnic groups that are non-Caucasian. Making America white is their goal .The Confederate criss-cross and the traditional Christian cross are the two symbols that make up the red, white and blue flag of the British Empire, who have immense white power. The Confederate flag is the banner of the Confederate conservative American. This flag is still being promoted today by many citizens who believe in federal terrorism and the supreme Confederate white man.

American Terrorism

The main sufferers of slavery and terrorism in America were the black folk who physically, mentally and spiritually were abused more than any other race in American history. I do admit that the Jewish genocide was extremely terrible, but here in America, the tyrants were white men who hid behind nice suits, military uniforms, and priestly robes. The Atlantic slave trade brought millions of black African men and women to white America to be slaves and barred from citizenship.

The Naturalization Act of 1790 forced Africans to work for free, build the entire country and be second class citizens. Extreme persecution was a daily event. Think about all the dehumanization that the African nation suffered at the hands of their oppressors in America and Africa.

In Africa and America the land of the free there were white only restrooms, white only restaurants, white only churches, white only neighborhoods, white only schools, white only sports, white only gas stations, white only jobs, white only this, white only that, there were even white only words. Mother was a white word. Black women who took care of masta's children were called mammies, not mothers.

Black women were treated like pets and some would kill themselves to rid themselves from the persecutions. Violence was viewed as a sporting event and white folk would make black folk fight each other all the way to death, even to the gouging out of eyes. This barbaric violence comes from their Greek, Roman, Homosapien, homosexual ancestors who used to watch their slaves battle gladiators and lions.

These bloody barbaric events happened in the Colosseum and tower of Babylon like structures. These violent events are what created sports and sports stadiums of today! White children learned from their dehumanizing parents and participated in the beatings and murders. They were educated and nursed into learning racial terror. The upper-class white southerner was confident that their race was superior to any other race. They were gentlemen, which was another white word.

The southern whites were noble, and they felt that they didn't have to work and figured that's why slaves were created. Such a horrifying conscience to abuse human life as if it's nothing. The religion Christianity was used to control black folk and this was accomplished by only revealing certain scriptures of obedience to masters, never scriptures of freedom and equality. Black folk was sold at auctions like real estate and cars, such a shame.

Some of the white man's wives would write diaries and share their feelings. They hated when their husbands would purchase beautiful black women because they knew that they would end up pregnant. One white woman wrote that she felt sorry for the black folk and would find it impossible for her husband, his friends and racist business partners to make it into Heaven.

The wives of these men still were dehumanizing to blacks like their spouses. When they had children, they would find one of the black women who just gave to breastfeed their child so they wouldn't have the responsibility. These black women would grow to love these children only to have them turn into evil replicas of their parents. If the child thought of being a sympathizer they soon learned of the repercussions of those thoughts. Black folk was terrorized by these European terrorists who have partaken in some of the most horrendous acts in all human history.

Black folk were drowned, pulled apart by horses and trees, set on fire, whipped, dismembered, hung, beheaded, dragged, shot, stabbed, strangled, robbed, raped {female and male}, crucified, beaten, spit upon, mutilated beyond description, tortured beyond conception. President Abraham Lincoln had a heart and stepped in to try and stop American terrorism and ushered in the 13th amendment.

I believe some of his peers and members of the Congress hated him for this which is why they placed on a brown copper penny turned an opposite way from the other coins. This symbolizes Lincoln taking a detour on racism to help black and copper color folk. It didn't matter because black folk continued to be slaves and victims of racism violating the 13 amendment, Emancipation Proclamation, Pledge of Allegiance and Declaration of Independence. Even after the signing of the Emancipation Proclamation and the victory of the civil war black folk were still oppressed.

Some people stated nothing changed after the civil war the persecutions just lightened up a little. I find that statement to be true because the same year being 1865 was a blind victory with the creation of the all-American terrorist group the Klu Klux Klan. This terrorist group was founded by a high ranking Confederate official who goes by the name of Nathanial Bedford Forrest, in Tennessee. This terrorist group grew to great heights in Indianapolis Indiana, which is why there will always be a racist spirit in that state.

Another founding father of this terrorist group was Minor Merriweather. His wife once said that the Klan was a miracle of God. They had freed their slaves previously but later felt that the former slaves would feel equal to the white folk, stripping them of their power. This man's wife praised the fact that these white men would put on white robes and hoods and pose as dead Confederate soldiers murdering and scaring black folk at their homes, in public, and at political polls.

Klansmen were so connected politically that they could get clearance to come in jails and take black men and murder them without being charged. These things continued since under the white hoods were police, senators, councilmen, doctors, judges and ex-slave owners.

There were other terrorist groups such as the Redshirts, Bulldozers, and the Cowboy. These groups assisted the white terrorist group the Klu Klux Klan. There were white Christian missionaries, abolitionist, Quakers and poor whites who were racially treated equally to black folk. These people helped black folk before and after the civil war. They also were tormented, beat, murdered and their houses were burnt down upon the discovery that they were Negro sympathizers. The land of the free America was a gigantic terrorist camp housing the African Nation as slaves creating a human franchise for the white man.

PART II **Fake** Economic **System**

Two Faced Politician

History records show that the Civil Rights Act of 1964 was supposed to one of the best things that happened to black America. President Lyndon Johnson endorsed this act, and he's looked at as a president that cared and supported the total freedom of black America but in reality, he was a two faced politician.

When Mr. Johnson became president after the assassination of President Kennedy, he would speak of the civil rights movement and lay claim to support Dr. Martin Luther King and the movement.

On the other side Mr. Johnson and the leader of the FBI Jay Edgar Hoover gave no protection for Dr. King. They were very deceitful and continually tried to get Dr. King caught up in scandals following him everywhere. When President Johnson was in the public, he would say good things towards Dr. King but in the company of his white peers, he would constantly call Dr. King niggers.

When Mr. Johnson was senator, he proposed the Civil Rights Act which was a great deal even though it took 87 years to come through the Senate. Once again I only speak the truth when I say that most of the white powered political leaders were white racists and hated black people with a passion. One of the haters and rejecters of the Civil Rights Act was none other than Senator President George Bush Sr. Kanye West didn't know that Daddy Bush didn't care about black people either.

The main reason I say President Johnson is a two faced politician, is because of what he said when he was a senator. On one side he told the Senate liberals, those who support freedom for blacks that the civil rights bill was quote "long overdue", but on the other radical southern Republican side, he said quote, "These Negroes, they're getting pretty uppity these days, and that's a problem for us, since they've got something now they never had before, the political pull to back up their uppityness. Now we've got to do something about this, we've got to give them a little something, just enough to quiet them down, not enough to make a difference."—LBJ (Wikipedia)

This recorded statement leads me to believe that the Civil Rights Act was just to shut black America up and blind their eyes from the economic New World Order slavery plan.

The plan that transfers plantation slaves to slaves of the government. Think about it; current President Obama may have been made president just to shut black America up. Something like a human form of the Civil Rights Act. Using Obama was a smart move. I believe the higher ups used him to give black America a sense of hope while ushering in new Acts, Orders, Bills, Treaties and Laws that are changing America. I will never say anything negative about Obama, but do you think that white racist leaders who hate black people would ok a black man as president without a hidden reason or agenda?

The white elites know things beyond your understanding so don't think for one second that a black president is evidence of positive change. The faces change but the racist motive always stays the same. Obama's adversary Mitt Romney is what some would also call a two-faced politician. He opposed welfare even though in the past his grandfather hit a bad spot and needed public assistance such as welfare.

Did you know more of white America is on welfare than black America?

Black America always gets the blame for all the negatives in government funded or lack of government funded programs. Black American's sovereignty is only half true. The Constitution and the Amendments were 1st created to support white America, then subsequently minority America. There will always be two sides to every story and in this case two faces. All of this is leading you to the fake American dream. Politics is another form of policing. By definition, it is the practice and theory of influencing other people. More narrowly it refers to achieving and exercising positions of government and organized control over a human community, particularly a state, more overly the world.

Understanding the Fake American Dream

'A dream is something that the subconscious mind envisions when a person is asleep.'

The American dream may be something that you're looking and hoping for but will never find because you have to be asleep to dream. The question is are you sleeping?

People have lived and died trying to achieve the American dream. I mean really what in the hell is the American dream? A white picket fence? A dog, big house, nice car, kids, great job, retirement, social security insurance, leaving something for relatives when you die?

If this is the American dream why are so many people in America living in hell, living the American nightmare? The American dream is nothing other than a fake fairytale-like the movie The Wizard of OZ. Understand that the god of this earth is the devil, and he is a fake, most of your dreams are fake, and when you wake up you may be still sleep trying to chase a dream that you'll never find.

It's something like the song named 'Fools Gold' by the talented recording artist Jill Scott. You may be living a dream believing things that just ain't true, and anything that's not true is a lie, but you still continue to chase this dream blind to the fact that your chasing gold that is gold plated.

---

*The American dream is just another
white lie.*

The reality is the economy itself is an illusion, and your true destiny is to die. Do remember the song row your boat gently down the stream? This song is so real because life is but a dream. Every day you live is a blessing and a dream because one day in the future no matter how healthy you may be, no matter how many diseases you may overcome, nor how much money you may have, you are going to die. This is 7+ billion people's reality.

The American dream is the white man's dream. They dreamed of an economic system of imperialism, capitalism, communism and they have millions of people believing in this fake ass dream. Picture this: Imagine if some catastrophic event destroyed the entire economic system on the earth. No shelter, no electricity, no clean water, no gasoline, no food supply and no communication. You would instantly turn into a primitive being. Your dreams would be dreams, and your reality would only be to survive, and you better have a bag of weapons, fire, food, and water. You should want to wake up.

Do you remember the movie the matrix? How Neo woke up and busted out of the bubble and found out that everything was fake? His name, job, and life, everything was fake! Let's explore the American dream. Let's start with money since that's what most people are focused on and so many people are killing and dying for it.

Fake Money

Water, fire, coal, soil, oil, electricity, energy, animals, humans, vegetation, minerals, precious metals, and stones, these things have monetary value.

Green paper money is fake! In the 1800's there was a gold and silver standard that sustained the economy. The gold standard was removed in the early 1900's and later in the 1960's during the Nixon era; the silver standard was removed. This was done so that the government could monitor all the money that is printed by the Federal Reserve.

This money system was coppied from previous European systems. The Germans and Americans experienced what could happen when the money system becomes exhausted which creates hyperinflation This occurred during the Great Depression era, and the reason bread, milk, and meat was the camount of a whole day's wages. Adolph Hitler became the Germans leader with promises to save the economy.

The Federal Reserve adopted this paper money system after the financial crisis from World War 1. All this system does is put the country in serious debt. The problem is there is nothing to back the money but promises and printing more money. This system allows currency, credit, debt and interest to come from thin air and it just grows and grows. This green paper money is made from white cotton and it's used to pay off trillions of dollars of debt to the Asian Triangle which consists of China, Korea, and Japan.

The Asian Triangle lends money and sells goods to the USA for much more than the strength and confidence in the American dollar. There are classified deals between the United States and China which are why they are both members of the Big 5 of the UN. The USA stays in debt from the corruption of the stock market, and many different privately owned institutions and organizations. This helps the lenders stay rich, and the borrowers stay poor.

The federal government is in control of the main banking institutions, so if the economy goes down, they have the power to inflate the currency, raise taxes or fall out which would be a disaster. The economy was going great in the roaring 20s. Everybody was working and had good jobs. The farming business was booming and all of a sudden the stock market crashed, and millions of shares were sold in one afternoon.

Men were insider trading; the rich became poor, and people were jumping out of windows and eating out of garbage cans. The Depression was in full swing. The new deal came in to save America, and the fake money system was born.

Fake Job

If you're not in the capitalist or upper classmen tax bracket, you are a working poor lower class slave. Think about it. When you first apply for a basic job you more than likely don't have any experience but you need the money so you apply. After convincing yourself you can break bricks in the boiling hot sun, you proceed to fill out an application. The questions contained within the application force you to tell the industrial slave master all your business. Your name, number, address, social, etc.

In the interview, you have to sometimes tell white lies about your experience and capabilities especially if you have a felony conviction or you won't even be considered employable. You then lie and confess out your mouth that you're happy to receive minimum wage, which equals the compensation of a 19th century slave.

After you're hired for the position you have to sign a contract and give 40 or more hours a week of your life to the white slave master, something like selling your soul to the devil. You have to get up at 5 in the morning, spend 10 dollars a day in gas and report to your white slave master. You have to deal with your master when he acts white. You have to act nice to other slaves that are racists.

You have to work with Uncle Tom slaves that kiss ass and they might tell master on you because they don't like you. On top of all this stress, you have to deal with your family who might not hardly see you because you have to put in so much overtime and you still don't have enough money to pay all the bills, so you stay drunk, high and in church.

One day you may come into work and the Uncle Tom slave is acting nice to you. You pay it no mind until the end of the day you receive a message from your supervisor to go see the slave master in the big boss's office, then you're fired.

Do you still think your job is real and you're not experiencing slavery?

Your position at your job is only half secure. You are being extorted every payday by the state and the federal government. You're brainwashed into thinking this is not a criminal act. If you pay child support through their system, they're getting a piece of that too. Child support is a white slave master system that was created by Congress in 1975, to ease the government responsibility to single mothers from receiving public assistance. Instead it has become a great career and cash cow for some single mothers who get mad at their ex husbands or boyfriends.

The system encourages single mothers to file charges on their child's father to receive income. Many fathers have been arrested for violation of this money system that makes billions of dollars in interest. This why the police will come arrest you and embarrass you anywhere for child support. You are forced to let them take your money and you can't do anything about it.

The government borrows money from your social security benefits that you worked many hard years to achieve so they can pay interest and debts owed to foreign countries. Your social security benefits are slowly vanishing and the federal government knows it. They are legitimately stealing. I guess you can do this if you're the boss.

Do you know your job can suddenly end no matter how much rank or history you have with your company? All it takes is for a greedy company to borrow money from super rich lenders, buy up all the stock from the target company, pay the premiums and then seek funds to pay back the lenders. They also so can move the company to a foreign region to make enormous profits in wage changes. Just like that you either would be fired, forced to take a pay cut or receive a severance package.

Your job is over and now you wanna jump out a window or kill your family. Lord have mercy. They were doing these things during the Great Depression and in the recent Recession. The federal government continues to try and stabilize the economy so that hyperinflation won't come pay a visit to our everyday lives. This inflation would make bread, milk and cheese very expensive. They hide these enormous debts in the rise of normal everyday expenses such as gas, food and lottery. Your desire to reach the fake American dream keeps you oblivious to the true state of the American economy.

Fake Name

There are millions of people on this planet that share the exact same name. People even name their children Jesus and I used to think it was only 1 man named Jesus. A name should identify you and only you and Jesus Christ in the Bible has this particular name! If you go to scripture and read Revelations 19:12 you will understand that even Jesus has a name that only he knows and it's not Jesus! It's a new name, a name greater than Jesus! If you read Revelations 2:17 you will understand that Jesus said that those who overcome will have a new name also! A name extremely greater than the name you have right now.

Understand that this world is a spiritual, bio chemical, electro-magnetic, digital, demonic white man matrix. It's controlled by numbers not names. The numbers make the name powerful or powerless. These numbers are really your name:

Social Security	ID or Driver License	Passport Number	Tax Id Number	Credit Score
Account Number	Confirmation Number	Pin Number	Address	Street Number
Phone Number	Password # Birth Certificate	Gallery Jail Number	Prison DOC Number	E-mail

These numbers identify who you are. They identify how much money you have, where you live, where you work, if you have children, if you are a convicted felon, if you have a warrant, if you have good credit, everything there is to know about you. Your social security number is another story.

Your signature on your social security number makes the government tremendous amounts of money so you're really born a millionaire, but your account is froze and owned by the Federal Government.
You probably know your social security number by memory but it doesn't even belong to you and it can be confiscated. It belongs to the Social Security Administration and it tells you this on the back of your social security card. There is a red 8 digit serial number that is your personal control number. The owners hold all the records, of the millions of people that were born the time and place you were born.

There is also an 8 digit number on green money that monitors all the billions of dollars that were made at that time and place. We are physical forms of cash money for the government. We are property of the United States Federal Reserve of America.

Social security is a systematical method of slavery, human enfranchisement and your signature binds you to this white racist slave master system. So what is the American Dream? I know one thing, it's time we wake up.

Compare the Economic Tornado to the Movie 'The Wizard of Oz'

In the process of developing a unique skill just being able to be silent, read and listen, I was reading a book and the famous fairytale The Wizard of Oz came on TV and grabbed my attention. I put my book down and began to watch this picture and could not believe what I was seeing and hearing.

I discovered the story has a hidden messages that describes many things in this book. This movie premiered in era of The Great Depression and the first year of World War 2. It was most famous because the movie started in black and white. When Dorothy opened the door and entered in the New World, the movie switched to color. This movie tells many stories about the many controversies and conspiracies of the American conquest. I will now share with you my theory.

The story starts off with a little white girl named Dorothy and her dog Toto. They're running down a dirt road in the city of Kansas. She's upset with this evil Christian woman because she keeps hitting on her dog. She gets home and tells her Aunt about this problem. The story doesn't say anything about her mother or father, so maybe they died or maybe she ran away, because she is a runner.

Her Aunt is too busy to pay Dorothy any attention because she's running a prosperous farm business. Three workers who work for her Aunt criticize Dorothy about her problem.

The first one tells her she needs a brain, so he thinks she's stupid. The second thinks she's a coward, so he says she needs to get some courage. The third one says that the town is going to make a statue out of him one day, so he doesn't even care and has no heart. She gets upset about their comments and tries to talk to her Aunt again about her problem. Her Aunt tells her she needs to go somewhere and stay out of trouble. Dorothy's now so hurt that she wishes she could go somewhere far away and starts singing about this distant place over the rainbow.

Later the evil Christian woman comes to the farm and threatens Dorothy with criminal charges because of accusations of a dog bite. Her Aunt restrains herself from cursing at this woman because the woman is a well-known lady of the community. The woman settles for taking the dog away from Dorothy. She takes the dog, but the dog escapes and runs back to Dorothy.

Dorothy and the dog then run away down the dirt road and they come up on a sign that says Professor Marvel and he's on a conquest to Europe. Conquest means control over a place or people by military force. This represents the European conquest that conquered America.

Professor marvel looks through crystal balls and predicts things about her running away. He says his crystal ball was used in the times of Osiris and Isis, the Black King and Queen. He looks through the ball and sees Dorothy's Aunt is upset because she left. Dorothy feels she needs to return home and then finds that the town is going through a terrible storm and there is a tornado that's tearing through the countryside. This tornado represents the stock market crashing.

Dorothy battles the strong winds and heads home to be with her family, but they have hid in the cellar. As much as she tries, Dorothy is unable to open the cellar door so she goes back in the house. In a flash of events the house begins to shake and Dorothy is hit in the head by a large piece of the bay window seal and she loses consciousness.

The tornado then takes the house into the air with a terrified Dorothy inside. She envisions the evil Christian woman riding a bike, and then she transforms into a green face witch now atop of a broom. The house then crashes to the ground and Dorothy wakes up nervous, scared and alone in a world so different from her small town. She gets up and walks towards the door.

In the roaring twenties the farm business was booming, people were living well and the economy was great. The Depression came and changed everything.

This is what this represents. When she opened the door she found that she wasn't in Kansas anymore. She was in a New World. A world full of color, vegetation and beautiful flowers. The land she was in was called Munchkinland and all the people in this entire movie besides the main characters and the ones in the city of Oz were little people, symbolizing how the powers that be feel about the common American.

The tornado that crashed the stock market brought the house down and it killed the witch of the east. The so called good witch Glenda appears out of a pink orb. She is the white pretty face witch who has power to teleport to certain events. She has a secret agenda to bring in the New World Order of the Federal Reserve Act and the New Deal. Her being the witch of the north tells you where she is dominate as in Europe and North America.

The wicked witch of the west appeared out of red smoke. She also has the power to teleport and she is the sister of the witch of the east whom the house landed on and destroyed. The wicked witch wanted retribution for her dead sister and vowed to get Dorothy.

The good witch taunted the wicked witch about the power of her dead sister's ruby slippers while magically placing them on Dorothy's feet. The good witch then scares the wicked witch by saying a house may fall on her, therefore she leaves. All Dorothy wants to do is go home and if the good witch was truly good, she would have advised Dorothy to use the power of the ruby slippers to go home.

Instead she tells her about the Great Wizard of Oz who in the old world was a sorcerer on a conquest through Europe. The wizard and the good witch represent the 16th century European conquest and the division of the continents. The good witch tells Dorothy to follow the yellow brick road to the wizard who can help her get home. The good witch ushers Dorothy into the New World Order, the Federal Reserve Act and the New Deal.

Dorothy represents America, the America that obeys the white man. Dorothy and her dog hop along and they come across a scarecrow, a tin man and a lion. These three are the same three that mocked Dorothy in the old world. The characteristics of the three are what the white powers feed off of. Ignorance, heartlessness and fear. The scarecrow needs a brain but he's walking. The tin man needs a heart but he cries. The lion needs courage but he walks upright. All three of them including Dorothy really have what they need but the good white witch has manipulated them and now has them on a mission to see a fake white wizard. Poor insecure Dorothy is so gullible that she believes anything the white witch tells her just like most Americans. They get closer to their destination and see an emerald city.

The wicked witch of the west monitors them from a crystal ball just like the sorcerer in the old world. She decides to create some poison poppies to stop them. She and her ex business partners the good witch and the wizard, distributed all the drug potions and witch magic across America.

The wicked witch made her own army by casting spells and turning her soldiers into brainwashed monkeys who fly, scream and cause terror upon her command. Dorothy and her crew start to run through the poppy field, they get sleepy and fall asleep. This represents the heroin that flooded America.

2

Glenda the good white witch causes it to snow and they wake up. This represents the cocaine that flooded America. The drugs that flooded America in the past was flooded by good and bad guys. Dorothy and the crew finally make it to the green city at the end of the yellow brick road. The end of the road is the end of the gold standard and the beginning of serial numbers and green paper. The city represents the green monetized money system of the Federal Reserve Act and the New Deal.

Dorothy rings the bell and knocks on the door of the beautiful green building and a man dressed in green appears at the door, saying state your business. They request to see the wizard and the man lies and says no one has never seen the wizard but changes his story when he finds out his business partner the good witch sent Dorothy. The man who really is the fake wizard, lets them in the green palace and they find a whole community of Americans. Their entire wardrobe is green including everything inside. This represents American green cash money.

They see the horse that changes 4 colors. The first color of course is white (white man). The second color is purple (power/royalty). The third color is red (war). The 4th color is yellow (gold). These are the 4 stages of the American conquistadors of Europe. The white man, has the power, and they make war, and take gold.

After they get cleaned up by the green working class Americans they arrive at another door. The same man tries not to let them in but after hearing Dorothy's sad story he leaves and the doors open. They finally make it to the wizard and he says he's all powerful and he is Oz. This represents the white leaders playing god.

Dorothy and the three make their requests to the fake wizard. He then starts talking trash to all of them and offers to grant their requests only if they sell their souls to him to do evil for him, something like a contract that allows you to kill people. He wanted them to kill the wicked witch and bring her broom to him. In return he would grant their wishes.

This wizard is a powerful con artist and makes promises that fall short just like the devil. They had to travel through a haunted forest and go to the witch's castle to complete this mission. This resembles the military. Military leaders have always commanded soldiers to go through forests to enemy lands to police something, take something or kill groups of innocent people. Soldiers have fought for the country by killing, stealing and destroying. This is the American way right or wrong. So they go through the forest and the first creature they see is an owl. This is one of the masonic symbols of the Illuminati-Freemasons.

They make it out of the forest after a few fights with the witch's military. Dorothy gets detained but eventually comes in contact with the enemy target. She engages a liquid agent and defeats the enemy and retrieves her broom. The green face leaders of the deceased witch's military decide to join the conquest and hail Dorothy's victory. Dorothy and the three head back to the green city to see the wizard.

After a small debate with the wizard, Dorothy's dog snatched back the curtain and they found out that the great wizard was a fake. He tried to tell a couple of white lies but then apologized for his actions. He grants their wishes by giving them medals to symbolize the things that they already had. Something to make them feel like they achieved something great but really didn't mean or do a damn thing. The wizard then says one of the committees of the university and the land that they were in was called E pluribus Unum!

This is clearly true Freemason Federal Reserve talk in the nation's favorite fairytale. The wizard then tells the story about how his balloon flew down to the land and the little people thought he was something like a god and made him the wizard. The fake wizard was about to grant Dorothy's wish and take her home in the balloon. Her dog caused another malfunction and he drifted away.

The so called good white witch appears after leading them to a fake, lying, manipulating, brainwashing man that caused them to commit a crime. She then tells Dorothy how to get home.
She says she didn't tell Dorothy how to get home at first because she wanted her to know the value of home. That lying witch. If you really think about it, Glenda and the wizard are the wicked witches and criminals in the movie. They are the ones who made threats, committed thefts, contracted murders and performed genocide to the east and west powers of the world. The witch of the west never committed any of these acts but she's the one who is called wicked.

Anyway, Dorothy clicks her heals three times and she teleports back in the old world that she wanted to get away from so bad. The new world looked good, but it was full of fakes and witches just like the real world. Not one black person was in this movie because 95% of Hollywood elites were white racists back then.

Barry Gordy created the production for The Wiz for Black America and created a different spin of the Economic Tornado. This movie showed you who the wizard really is in real life, a lying politician! In the end of this movie the message was for freedom, happiness, independence and a brand new day for African American people who were looked at as slaves.

This movie has great actors, comedians and major recording artists that were all ages and different sizes, much different from the white Wizard of Oz. There was even beautiful babies in this movie showing the difference of the heart of the black man and of the white man. They're both great fairy tales that tell the story of the Economic Tornado.

PART III Science Knowledge & Colors

Unveil Their Secrets

This world is very mysterious. It's filled with 7 continents, beautiful islands, oceans, seas, rivers and many other bodies of water. There is plant life, animal life and they have different classes, sizes, shapes and colors. The two most common animal classes consist of reptiles and mammals. I will reveal mysterious knowledge about the reptile in a future chapter but right now I'm focused on the most complex mammal who are the gods of this earth, the humans. I want you to think about all the different nationalities, races, colors, classes and creeds for a minute ok?

There are Africans, Asians, Europeans, Mexicans, Puerto Ricans, Russians, Brazilians, Egyptians, Ethiopians, Indians, Koreans, Palestinians, and Arabians to name a few. You may be reading this book and you may be very intelligent but I'm very sorry to inform that you are brainwashed and somewhat influenced to be stupid when it comes to race relations.

The intelligent school teachers whoever they are teach us that we are colors. Their intelligence and strength is nothing when it comes to the knowledge of the Lord. This is the reason why I use many Bible verses to reveal truths.

With that thought let us go to 1st Corinthians 1:25, which says the foolish things of God are wiser than human wisdom and the weakness of God is stronger than human strength. With this scripture in mind you will understand

*God's foolishness is really infinite wisdom
and man's wisdom is really infinite
foolishness*

That would mean that some of the most intelligent men on this earth are really ignorant fools and don't know a damn thing. The real nature of things are totally opposite to what the common human sees or believes. So the good things you believe to be true and good, may really be false and evil. The people you believe to be good and resemble angels, may really be evil demonic satanic devils.

Now returning to the different nationalities, tell me why among all these different classes of billions of people upon the face of the earth, there are only two that identify themselves as colors? These two of course are Europeans and people of African descent. The black and white.

These two colors even act as nouns and adjectives when it describes a person, place or thing. One would say he or she acts black or that he or she acts white. A white person can even act black and a black person can act white. A place can be black or white, as well as one can dress black or white or talk black or white. Crime can be black or white as well as music. One thing I know for sure that's black and white is a piano, a penguin and a zebra.

Why can't an Indian person look red, act red and be called red? Why can't a Mexican look tan, act tan and be called tan? Why can't an Asian man look yellow, act yellow and be called yellow? They can't. Even though these are the same scenarios with different classes of people, your mind can't register to call any other nationality a color but two. We are all somewhat brainwashed to address a human being as a color. Europeans and those of African descent can look black or white, act black or white and be a black or a white. These two colors will always be at war over many different circumstances and situations.

The influence of racism was placed in all aspects of science, knowledge and colors. Therefore a white man will always be considered a good guy and a black man will always be considered a bad guy, a low down thug and a hard core criminal. The white man will constantly be possessed with pride because it's implanted inside their brains and belief systems. The constant hatred of the black man is an inherited curse from the devil.

The devil is a liar and the white man lies and says he's white. We all have melanin that makes up our various skin tones but we are not colors. We are people!

Black

Open your mind while I explain the most important color in life. The color is black and even if you hate this color, after you read this chapter topic you will understand that you've been hating a color that is part of you, no matter what color you think you are. You must come to the understanding that everything is black, was black and will always be black.

Black is the beginning and ending of everything

The color that was before the colors in the color spectrum was black. Before the Big bang, when the Creator made the first day it was first black. The universe is still black and even if it would blow up, it would have to go back to black to be created again. The most mysterious energy is black. The most powerful force that has the power to swallow light is black. The white judges who convict billions of people wear robes that are black. The soil that grows everything on this earth is black. The longest river in the world is black. The first humans on the earth were black. The most common hair color in the world is black. Almost every tire on every car is black. Almost every street across the world is black. Almost every TV, computer and phone across the world is black.

Before you were alive you were unconscious to the flesh so your life was black.

On the day that you die you are going back to the black. When family and friends go to your funeral, they're more than likely going to wear black. The pen ink that has written every major document and contract in history is black. The highest level in martial arts is black. The president of white America 2008-2016 is black. The cars that he and his governmental entourage ride in are black. The suits that the most powerful people wear in the world are black.

Before money was green it was gold and it was owned by men who were black. Most of the masonic symbols were first black. To come to the light first everything in your life must go black. So all this interesting information about black but when it is defined in the dictionary, black is evil, bad, miserable and unhappy.

Black people compliment this definition because they're commonly defined as powerless, nothing, and useless even though black people have invented some of the most extraordinary devices and formulas in history. How can you embrace the color black, explore black and elect a black president but hate black people at the same time? This is how you know racism and brainwashing has been placed in this powerful color when it comes to black and black people. As Jay Anthony Brown would say, "Damn white people."

White

Open up your mind while I explain the color white and why the Europeans use this color for their description. When you're a white man you're automatically considered right, honest, smart and a good guy. Of course every opposite of the good white man would be the bad black man who is always considered wrong, a liar, ignorant and a bad guy.

There is serious personification issues to assume one is good or bad just from a color. If the white man is all good then why don't white judges wear white robes? The word white is defined as clean, holy, true, innocent, pure, unblemished, life and blameless. All of these are great things. These definitions relate to the attributes of the Most High God.

The word white that is used in most standard dictionaries must be describing another word because white things on this earth cause bad things to happen that might lead to death!

White Salt =high blood pressure, heart attack, death
White Sugar=diabetes, heart disease weight gain, rotten teeth
White Bread=digestive problems, bloating, weight gain
White Castle=upset stomach, death smelling gas
White Cocaine=addiction, prison, death
White Meth=addiction, prison, death
White Pills=addiction, prison, death
White Lands=oppression, prison, death
White Supremacists=oppression, prison, death
White Police=oppression, prison, death
White Women of the past=oppression, prison, death
White Priest=oppression, rape, prison, death
White Judges=oppression, prison, death
White Laws=oppression, prison, death
The White House= white laws, white lie's and confusion

Not one human on the face of the earth is the color of snow, sugar or more over the color white. So Master Webster and other dictionaries have the world believing something that is not true and this is also white and is called a white lie!

This would define white as appearing clean but really unclean. Appearing holy but really unholy. Appearing true but really untrue. You can't believe everything you see or hear and too much of anything white just might kill you. Even when you die, they say your skin turns white or pale. Being white and turning white doesn't always mean you're right. Sometimes it just might mean the total opposite.

Turn in your Bible to the book of Numbers 12:1-16 and you will read that skin that turns white is a curse and there was something evil or deceitful done for this color change to happen. In this chapter you will read that Moses's sister spoke against him because he married an Ethiopian wife. She made God very angry and He turned her skin white. In the book of 2 Kings 5:20-27, Elisha's servant turns white for trying to get material gain by deceitfulness. This curse was upon him forever.

The white curse of power, deception and death is described in the book of Revelation 6:2-8. This scripture speaks of the unknown rider upon a white horse conquering the world, who in the end the identity of the rider is revealed and his name is death. The white man is the devil.

Red White and Blue

The red, white and blue connects to nations across the world in more than 21 countries. These are the colors of their banners of honor. Different flag but all have the same colors. Other than the obvious color palette, these flags share the commonality of representing white supremacy and influence.

The color red is first because it represents the blood that has been spilled for the superiority of the true white man. The color white is second; it controls both colors. The color blue is last representing the blue water that was sailed by the white man to create slavery and democracy in America. These three colors represent people who fight against each other never knowing the real cause of the conflict but being controlled by the color white.

The color wars are between two rival gangs called the red and blue political parties. The G.O.P, Good ole party is the Republican Party represented by red, and their mascot is a giant elephant representing white power.

The Democratic Party is blue, and their mascot is a Jackass, who represents the gullibility of the impoverished to accept the lack of education as their penance and turn a blind eye to the wrongs committed against them by others. You are encouraged by your white government to become a member of one of the red or blue parties and become a red or blue person, even though you may be a black or a white person. You are influenced to become red or blue because when you do that you become green cash for them.

In the street life you can also be a red or blue person when you become a member of one of the red or blue parties. Red is the color of the parties the Bloods and the Vice Lords. They are peeps and people who fight and war against cousins and folks. They are Crips, Gangsters, and Disciples, and they are the parties that are blue.

These red and blue political parties in the streets are at war, and the white man benefits from both color parties when some of their members go to jail and prison. The color wars in the streets are the exact same wars that are going on in regular politics except you're not fighting with guns in politics, you're fighting with your voice and votes. You express your loyalty to the red and blue brotherhoods every time you confess you're a Republican or a Democrat.

The color war of red, white and blue is more than what you think, even God and the devil are associated with colors. The blue sapphire is the color of the throne of the Lord reference Ezekiel 1:26 10:1 and the red ruby is one of the jewels of Lucifer in Ezekiel 28:13 and of course his traditional red dragon description in Revelation 12:3

All I know is the colors red, white and blue scare the hell out of you if you see them flashing in your rear view mirror!

So do these colors represent something good or something evil? One thing for sure, I know you pray to God or cuss if you see the red, white and blue lights in your rearview mirror. This is because you fear these three colors. These colors do not set you free, they enslave you and send you straight to jail and in the land of the living, jail is hell!

These colors are the law of the land and the continents of the world hold their red, white and blue banners up high in the air. This is evidence of the world wide power of the white man who polluted the world's perception of colors.

If you are a Caucasian or an African American you are a color. If you're in a political gang you are a color. If you're in a street gang you are a color. Colors describe who you are riding with and if you're not the right color you just might be the enemy. You are at war and you didn't even know it.

Humans

The word that describes who we are is human. After investigating this, you will understand that all of us humans are a separate species from the white man. The word human is composed of two words, hue and man. Hue means color and man means the human male. So human means color man. If you turn in your Bible in Genesis 2:7, you will read that man was created from the dust of the ground.

Humus is dark organic soil of decayed animal and plant life, substances of which man was created. So all these years that the white racist men were calling black men colored, they were describing the definition of a human being. So these white man were not human then right? They didn't call themselves colored men or niggers, they called themselves white men. They say man came from the black and brown ape, this would be the black human right?

*Non-human white man could have come
from the pink pig?*

The first two syllables in the word pig-men-ta-tion secretly reveal who these non-human white men might be, pig-men. This would explain the bologna smell or the wet dog smell that comes from some of their sweaty white bodies. Pork is forbidden by many religions and it causes the body to have many health problems. If you look at eating pork like eating a bologna smelling white man you might slow down on the pig. The white man must be another species because he sure isn't a colored man. That's what human means.

All of God's creations share a place in and out of the color spectrum but the white law was that the black man was colored. The white man separated himself from the color spectrum. They are the white man not the hue-man.

In the Bible there were angels who had the appearance of brass, amber and copper. In the book of Daniel 10:6, Ezekiel 40:3 and Revelations 1:15, you will read that Jesus and these angels were also colored. So would these racist white man think Jesus and these angels were niggers?

In the 21st century white folk go to tanning booths to get their skin darker and they go to surgeons to get their lips and buttocks bigger. After all the persecutions and cutting off noses and lips on African/Asian like structures across the world, now white people wanna darken their skin trying to look like people hated for so many years.

The former president of the NAACP received color change procedures and she swore that she was black, although she was conceived by white parents. She received a serious backlash for telling all her white lies.

Why are white folk trying to look like those whom they despise?

Probably because once upon a time we all were hue-mans. But who am I? I'm only a messenger.

PART IV Angels, Aliens, Demons

Michael vs. Lucifer

Angels are the personification of morning stars and suns. They are here to guard us and guide us. They guard us from evil and guide us to light to see the correct path. They are described as flames of fire, winds and flashes of lightning. Angels are supernatural messengers. I want to now discuss the leaders of the angelic world under the Most High. One of these angels is good. The other one is the total opposite. This is the Biblical revelation of the two chief commanders.

In the beginning of creation the Creator brought forth the energy force that created everything. This force created things at an innumerable time before our time. Advanced beings were created in these times and they were born before flesh. These creations were super beings, angels and Arch angels.

The first and the second most powerful angels were the two Arch angles Michael and Lucifer.

First you have to acknowledge the mighty Archangel Michael who people fail to realize how important he is to the entire Christian community. If you have a Bible concordance near you will find that the name Michael means like God. This is because Michael is the chief commander, captain and leader of all humans and all angels!

In your Bible in the book of Joshua 5:13-15, there is a captain and commander of the Lord's host who spiritually assists Joshua in the falling of Jericho's walls. Again it is written in your Bible in Daniel 10:13 that Michael the chief prince, came to help another angel fight demonic forces. Again in Daniel same chapter verse 21, that same angel tells Daniel that it is written in the Book of Truth that no one helps angels but Michael who is also Daniel's Prince.

This means that he is humanities prince also. In Daniel 12:1, the Bible states that in the end of time there will be a tribulation like never before in the history of the earth and Michael will stand up as a guard for the children of the people of earth. Ok now think, who does this great Archangel sound like? Are you listening? There's more.

In your Bible in the book of Jude 1:9, the Archangel Michael is in court contending with the Archangel Lucifer about the Law of Moses. This means that Michael defends humanity as a lawyer against the chief prosecutor. In Revelation 12:7, Michael and His Angels fought against the reptilian dragon Lucifer and his demonic angels. The dragon and his angels were kicked out of Heaven and thrown down to the earth by Michael. Ok again I ask you using 3rd grade Bible knowledge. Who does this Archangel Michael sound like? Let me run it down so you can get it.

All the angels in Heaven are his, he helps them fight, he helps humans fight, he's the only one that helps angels, he is their prince, he is humanities prince, he stands in court as a lawyer and judge in the spirit world for humanity, he stands up as a guard for the human children of the world, he will stand up for all of the children of the world in the end of the world and he kicked Lucifer and his angels out of Heaven! If you can receive it, the Archangel Michael is the spirit force that is Jesus Christ! Pay Attention!

The book of Matthew 24:1-51 talks about the same Great Tribulation in the book of Daniel. Jesus tells the entire story and even quotes the book of Daniel in verse

15. These are the beginning of the end times of the earth and Jesus talks about kingdoms and nations fighting each other, wars, rumors, earthquakes, starvation, chemical pollution, hatred, hate crimes, imprisonments, tortures, murders, family murders, martyrs, fake priests and prophets, even a fake Jesus who will do wonders that will brainwash millions of people.

All of these things begin when the world reverts back to the times of Noah. We are living in these times now if you pay attention. This scripture goes on to say that this Great Tribulation will bring the coming of the Son of man. He will appear as a flash of lightning coming for his righteous servants who will be caught up and transported out of space. Jesus will come in the clouds with His Angels shouting with the voice of the Archangel, sounding off the trumpet.

Jesus's voice is the voice of the Archangel Michael. This particular scripture was written centuries after the book of Daniel which was recorded before Jesus's earthly birth. This scripture tells the same description of what Michael will do in the end of time during the same Great Tribulation! The angels coming in the clouds with Jesus were first fighting under Michael before Jesus came into the flesh. The spirit is a force that is contained in a body. Jesus even said that the spirit of the prophet Elijah who ascended to Heaven, is John the Baptist. According to Jesus he was the greatest prophet that ever lived! Luke 7:28

If you ever read the book of Enoch you would find that it goes into great detail about Heavenly things. One of the most important things in this book is this secret name that the Ancient of Days made that only Michael the Archangel knew. This name which could be no other name but Jesus, bonded all the mysteries of wisdom and godliness together and it was in the instrumentality of Michael the Archangel. This was an extraordinary piece of information so much that the other angels pressed Michael hard to reveal the mystery.

The curious angels decided to leave their Heavenly estate by swearing and making oaths to bind themselves to a lower estate. They were kicked out of Heaven and then traveled to earth manifesting themselves in flesh. They had sex with human females procreating making children. These fallen angels taught the children of earth violence, how to kill, how to make weapons, how to make drugs from trees and the magical power of beauty.

They were all under the command of their leader and god Lucifer, whose name means son of the morning. He is the fallen bright and morning star which is what millions of people call Jesus Christ today, because He is also a bright star in fact He is the brightest.

Lucifer's light was very beautiful and he was covered with every precious stone. This is in Ezekiel 28. So don't think if you're tempted by the devil that the temptation will be nasty, dirty, smelly, ugly, evil and scary looking with horns. This Hollywood description of the devil is not how he or she would appear to you.

Lucifer would appear to you beautiful and wonderful to tempt you and would be trying to offer you something you desire like fortune, fame, sex, money, drugs or a contract. He tried to offer Jesus riches and kingdoms during the temptation in the wilderness in return for Jesus to bow down and worship him. Bowing down and prostration to God is true worship which Jesus refused to do. He defeated the devil with the Word which is what Jesus is.

The angel Lucifer became full of pride because of his/her beauty and coveted God. He also has a serious conflict of interest with the kingship of the hue-man race. He refused to submit to the total will of God. All these things led the Most High to convict Lucifer and his angels. This barred them from the inner courts of the sanctuary of Heaven.

Seeing that he fell he went to make war against God by corrupting the creation. He lives to tempt and torture the children of God, betting God that they will curse Him to His face. Obedience to the voice of the fallen one created death. The fallen nature was born making the creature the god of this earth.

The Reptile

I Seriously questioned my religion after reading the mind boggling book by the author David Icke. His book the Biggest Secret, goes into great detail about the white reptilian, white power government influencing all politics, Roman Catholic Christianity and almost every major economical operation on the face of the earth.

If it had not been for my faith there's no telling what I would believe.

After my complex biblical, scientific and social searching's, I have found many scriptures in the Bible confirming a reptilian presence and the worship of the reptilian god. If you turn your Bible to John 3:14, you will find that Jesus says that the reptile is the one who was lifted up as god instead of himself.

As it is written: "Moses lifted up the serpent in the wilderness, even so must the Son of man Christ Jesus be lifted up." The wilderness, every human being is going to sooner or later go through the wilderness. Even Christ himself went through the wilderness to be tempted by the devil. The world is the wilderness. The biblical definition of the wilderness is a deserted an empty hot dry place. The devil is the creator of the wilderness.

This is written in the book of Isiah 14:17. In the wilderness the prophet Moses was told by God to set up a bronze serpent to heal the children of Israel, who were bitten by serpents. The Lord sent the serpents to bite them after they were talking crazy about bread and water, reference the book of Numbers 21:5-9. Anyone who gazed upon this serpent was healed.

This reptilian symbol currently stands for life, death, medicine, viruses etc. This symbol is displayed in hospitals and on all medical doctor documentation and anything dealing with medical support. Pay attention to your local news station when they report health issues and you will see the serpents.

The serpent with wings on the pole, is the hero and savior for the United States of America and other countries as well. This symbol is registered by the American Medical Association and the Medical corps of the United States Army. The historic mythological reptilian snake is called Caduceus and is associated with the Greek god Hermes.

This symbol is the reptilian god. This is a Christian country and most Christians think Jesus is God.

Why isn't the symbol of healing something that compliments Jesus?

A tree, plant, flower, fruit, fish or most definitely a cross! It's not because it is written that Satan is the ruler and god of this world and this came out of the mouth of Jesus Christ in John 14:30. The white powered supporters and worshipers of the reptilian god lift him up as the healer, giver of life and the savior for the world.

Snakes, serpents, dragons and vipers are mentioned multiple times throughout the Bible for a reason. Take not lightly what is described in the Bible with clear English, letting you know that there is integration with the reptile. The book of Genesis explains the beginning of the reptilian influence.

In the Garden of Eden the chief fallen angel in the physical form of a reptile, seduced the woman who was unclothed and she tempted the man who was also unclothed. They both ate the fruit from the forbidden tree of Knowledge. Immediately after this their eyes were opened and they became conscience of what just happened. This event happens in Genesis chapter 3.

God asked the woman what she has done. He never asked Adam what he has done because he hasn't done anything. Eve says that the serpent beguiled her. Beguile means seduce, attract, enchant, hypnotize or mesmerize. Mind you this serpent was extremely beautiful and attractive. God curses the serpent and says He will put enmity between the serpent's child and Eve's child. Enmity means hatred or hostility.

God then announces that the serpent child will bruise Eve's child's heel and Eve's child will crush the serpent child's head, inflicting the fatal wound. God never spoke to Adam about having children only to Eve and the serpent.

So if you consider the first human child murdered the second child and consider two men can have a child by the same woman, then consider that the chief fallen one made a child who started the origin of jealously, anger, violence and murder. Creating offspring was the main purpose of all the fallen angels and now offspring are all over the entire earth. It isn't a secret.

Understand that we are all infected with the curse of being somewhat reptilian. The evidence is inside all of our heads in the back of the brain and it's called the Amygdala, the reptilian brain.

Remember in the gospels it is written in Mathew chapter 23:33, Jesus told the scribes and Pharisees that they were serpents and a generational offspring of vipers. This continual effect of the reptile has worked its way from the beginning of time all the way up to present day.

In classic mythology, astrology and astronomy, the 12 zodiac signs doesn't promote its 13th member. The zodiac constellation never mentions Cetus and Ophiuchus. Cetus is the giant dragon like sea monster and Ophiuchus is a star group which pictures a man holding a snake up high.

The constellation Draco describes a reptilian dragon and this star group led to the creation of the Draconian and also movie creations of Dracula and vampires. There are really reptilian vampires that walk the earth. They love drinking blood especially from young children. It is rumored that the royal reptilians have the power to shapeshift to disguise their true form. The royals are not green like most reptiles, they are white! White devils.

White Devil Domination

The book of Revelations chapter 6 tells the entire story of the white devil domination and it tells it in full detail. This chapter talks about the 7 seals but the first 4 describe the domination of the white devils. A seal is something that's concealed or hidden. It's information that is forbidden or held back from the public view.

There were 4 angelic creatures: A *lion* representing the true king whose crown is eternal after the tribe of Judah; a *calf* representing the human sacrifice; a *man* representing a true judge who will judge justly and fairly over mankind; an *eagle* representing the resurrection.

These 4 creatures ushered the prophet John to the visions that told the story of the white devil domination. The Lamb of God Jesus Christ is the only being that was found worthy to open these seals.

The 1st creature who told the prophet John to come look and see the vision was in the form of a lion, representing the true king whose crown is eternal. He is the lion after the tribe of Judah. The first seal is broken by the Lamb of God and the vision reveals an unnamed rider on a white horse, symbolizing white power. This rider was given a crown, a bow and he went riding through the earth conquering.

When I first read this scripture long ago I thought this was an angelic follower of God. This rider only has one crown, later in Revelations 19:11-14, Jesus is riding on a white horse with his heavenly army. They are also riding white horses and Jesus has many crowns because he is more than a conqueror. The one crown rider whose name is not mentioned is the king of the evil spirit world. He possesses the world with white power. He is the one who looks clean but is a low down filthy dirty wet dog, riding a beautiful white horse conquering with religion and weapons.

The 2nd creature who told the prophet John to come view the vision was in the form of a calf, representing the sacrifice for mankind. The Lamb of God breaks the second seal and it revealed a red horse, symbolizing bloodshed, war and murder. Its unnamed rider was given a great sword and given power to take peace from the earth so that people will kill each other. Quadrillions are destined to death by this demonic rider and by the hand of fellow brothers and sisters. Lord have mercy.

The 3rd creature who told the prophet to come look was in the form of a man, representing a true judge who will judge justly and be fair to mankind. When the Lamb of God broke open the third seal it revealed a black horse, symbolizing black power and judgement. The rider of this horse is also unnamed and he was given some scales and balances.

This rider uses these instruments to weigh things incorrectly and charges mankind too much for everything. This rider is the judge who convicts and punishes people harshly, judges unjustly and continues to profit and enjoy the fruits from the economic industry, devouring up all the fruits of the land.

The 4th creature who told the prophet John to come look was in the form of an eagle, representing the resurrection of the Overcomers. The Lamb of God breaks open the fourth seal. This one is different from the other 3 seals. This seal revealed a pale horse and its rider's name is mentioned, matter of fact this rider has two names. The two names of this rider are death and hell. This rider is carrying the curse of death and hell through the earth.

These 4 horses reveal the past, present and future powers that rule and persecute the people of the earth in the unseen world and in the world that's seen. If you compare this with the European conquest of America, you will see all of the similarities. These events are what led the world to be in the condition that it is today. White devil power.

Aliens

Do you believe in aliens? Some of you will say yes some of you say no. I personally do believe that there are other lifeforms, dimensions, planets and existences that are already present but some have yet to be discovered and understood by the general public. For those of you who don't believe that aliens exist and you believe in God, Jesus and the Bible, how can you say you don't believe?

In the Bible there are many unbelievable and unexplainable things. There is a talking snake, a talking donkey, a talking dragon, talking thunder and lightning, a talking tornado, talking sky, and a talking burning bush. There is fire that falls from the sky, clouds and fire guide people day and night. There is a fire breathing dragon, giants, beings with wings, beings that appear and disappear, flying horses, fire flying chariots, flying circular spaceships, flying angels, flying serpents, angels with 4 faces, men glowing like light, men that appear to be metal, dead men rising to life, men who have physically ascended out of space, men walking on water, water that heals diseases, emerald cities with pure gold streets, and many other things the average human being would call crazy.

Oh, I forgot you don't believe there are aliens but you believe all this other impossible sounding stuff in the Bible, ok whatever. If angels came down from

Heaven they would be considered aliens right? Heaven is really space where the stars are located.

An alien is a foreign person that comes to a land or neighborhood that is not theirs. If you were to see aliens, you would wonder who they were and why they came to visit your land. After I explain, you will know and understand that the aliens are here and not awaiting a visit. There are millions of reports and records of alien visits, abductions and spiritual possessions.

There may be thousands of different kinds. You may have heard of the Andromeda, Annunnaki, White Martians, Tall Whites, Reptilians and Greys. Some of these aliens are demonic entities that have visited our natural world claiming to be God.

If you want some supposedly authentic alien footage the movie's the Entity and the 4th Kind, will most definitely educate you on this subject. During these alien demonic possessions children and adults have reportedly levitated, seen white owls, seen UFO's, changed their voices, spoke in other languages, changed their faces, walked up walls, some have been thrown across rooms by invisible entities, some have had limbs break, some have been raped, some have been pulled through houses never to return and some have died.

These bizarre events began when one identifies unnatural things like a rearranged room, temperature changes, and an unusual spurt of anger, electronic disturbances or an unusual amount of flies, locust, birds or bats in the area. Some of these things are similar to the plagues in the book of Exodus. One of these events happened to a black family in the state of Indiana. That is very strange because these mysterious things usually happen to white people for some reason.

Other aliens have been reported to abduct humans and then return them after doing painful experiments and cross breeding. If this is true this would mean that there are half breeds walking upon the earth right now.

There are also stories that there may be billions of aliens that have come to earth to cross breed their DNA strand and confiscate natural resources and elements like atomic gold, diamonds and other materials to help rebuild themselves, their planet or create a new world. They reportedly trade higher up technology and chemical formulas to the government for these resources. The government then uses this knowledge to create advanced machines, medicines, diseases, viruses, weapons and projects to brainwash people to further the world domination operation.

Who do these aliens sound like?

If you want a simple version of aliens, just take a look at history and study the European Conquerors. Just think about it, they're the only ones that have used the exact same methods and have done the exact same acts as the reports of aliens.

They traveled from distant lands Europe and landed at new lands to conquer, trick and trade Africa and Asia. They approached the leader and offered business deals. The leader probably never seen a white man in his life so he immediately considered the white man as god and his people would assume the same.

If there was a dispute with these business deals murder would be the answer for refusal. The white man aliens had advanced weapons so warrior weapons like spears and swords were no match. Trading posts were set up and then the word colonize was born. Such a dirty word meaning control of a people's land by a foreign alien government. After the people were bribed their land was confiscated. Their furs, their gold and their livestock was taken. They were then abducted and transported to other lands to become slaves.

The people experienced hard labor, persecutions, brutal rapes and then the cross breeding began, creating various mixed races. There were also experiments conducted which transferred diseases and viruses to the captives during this process. The people contracted Cancer, Syphilis, HIV, Ebola and AIDS from the white man alien experiments.

This operation was then taken to other continents and the process begins all over again, all in the name of white Jesus. This is the true alien conspiracy for those you who don't want to believe the other high tech versions. History records show that the only alien that has invaded the earth, is the alien white man.

PART V Powers of the Air vs Family Life
The Apple=Computer 666

The craftiest device in the power of the air is the computer. It is the chief electronic communicator and giver of information. The biblical account of Genesis tells the story of the first tree of knowledge which was the apple tree. Obviously there was hidden knowledge that the Creator did not immediately want mankind to know, especially not to be ushered in by a fallen angel.

Man-kind was convicted to death and lead out of the Heavenly garden and brought down to the earthly dimension. All this from eating a sweet juicy apple? We really don't know if it was an apple that caused this terrible curse but it sure is the symbol. This symbol is currently the symbol of the computer and American Technology Company called Apple, confirming a connection to the book of Genesis and the forbidden fruit.

Computers were invented throughout the early 1900's in an effort to eliminate many processes of calculating and producing information. The computer is the post industrial revolution of technology that has advanced the entire human existence. Computers now run the world and smart phones have become just as powerful, because they too are mini computers.

The problem with these computers is that inappropriate information is available for children to access. Children can search different sites and play games that deal with murder, guns, drugs, porn or anything else that they become curious to google. These things should not be readily available for children.

Children are not born sinners like most preachers say. Children are born into a sinful world and then they may become sinners. In the gospels Jesus tells us that the only way that people will enter in the kingdom of God, is to become like a child free from pride. Children learn to sin from parents, friends, TV, radio and the computer.

New York is called the big apple. That leads me to believe that there are a lot of forbidden things happening in New York. The U.S. stock exchange is the very large computer residing in this forbidden apple. The computer is the sign of the mark of the beast and 666 is the number.

This number connects to the first Apple computer which retailed for $666.66. The scripture Revelation 13:15-18 explains this number and there is a small exercise you can do to show how deep this really is.

Spell out the alphabet from A- Z

Write down the number of the beast/man which is the number 6 under the letter A and continue adding 6 until you reach Z, so A would be 6 and B would be 12 C would be 18 and so on. Spell out the word computer and add up all the numbers with the letters.

What did you come up with? Is it a coincidence or is it truth revealed.

If you use the same mathematical method for the words Us of America, New York, Kissinger, Nuclear Hell and The Federal Reserve, you will find that these words also equal the number of the beast. The computer

*and the other 5 are the big 6 components of
the New World Order. A New World that's
ordered by the 6.*

The computer has ushered in mind manipulation, eavesdropping, wiretapping, drones and it is the major tool of the New World Order and the future electronic money system, the microchip implant, digital mind manipulation, the robotic revolution and transhumanism. The computer sends out thousands of messages to our mind every day and there are no filters. People pay more attention to their phones and computers than their own children. People sleep with their phones in the bed with them like teddy bears.

The computer has allowed porn to open up the mind to see immoral disgusting sex as inviting and normal. Normal sex used to be an experience between a man and a woman. Now sex with the same sex is inviting and normal by the law of man. Sex with teens and children are the most desired by internet porn users. Sex with dogs, horses, cows, pigs and other animals are often frequently desired and watched.

90% of the entertainers in child and beastiality pornography are for some reason white people. Will there be a day when it's lawful for man's best friend to be his boyfriend or girlfriend? Unfortunately it's probably here already.

The phone and computer have become the central tool for life. Look around the next time you're on a bus, subway, store, bank, nightclub, church, school or any other place of business. You will find that people interact more with their phone then they do with each other. There is hardly any natural socializing even dating has become computerized. You can lie and post pictures like you're a beautiful woman but when you meet this beautiful woman in person she might not have any teeth and she might have a penis. Catfishing or lying about your true self has become the normal practice for mainstream America.

The phone and computer have taken control of the mind and every aspect of a person's ordinary day. The events that take place are recorded and broadcasted for all the world to see. Work flow, church flow, school flow, club night, date night, fight night, family life, look at me, like me, selfie, RIP, look at this, I'm eating here, I'm there, I'm everywhere. All visual and verbal networks connect to promote wherever you go, whatever you do, whatever you say and whatever you can possibly think about... You become a human reality show.

The phone and computer have become society's god. Just ask the phone any question through google voice or iPhone's Siri and it will give you the answer. Everything is offered and everything is available just push search or go. We are eating many forbidden apples everyday and the children are even eating more. There are no restraints in place to protect the children and no one cares.

Hypnosis, brainwashing and mind control explains what some of us are experiencing on these computers and electronic devices. People are turning into robots being controlled by their electronic slave masters.

People believe anything master computer says. Sometimes you should turn off the computer and phone and try to experience a clear mind and a consciousness of oneself, the world and face to face communication. The powers of technology make it hard because it influences all levels of telecommunication.

Television

Television was an experiment after World War 2 and it became popular having the power to control. It is the seed that sprouted into the computer. Silicon Valley is where TV began in America and it became one of the chief powers of the air. It surpassed the radio because of the fascination of being able to hear and also see the vison making television 3 dimensional.

Television teleports visions to your mind. The visions that come from watching TV send electromagnetic signals to your mind so that you become hypnotized and controlled. The more time you spend watching TV, the more programming you will receive. Your mind connects and communicates with the television programs. When you become interested in the subject matter, TV becomes part of your daily life.

The television is an electronic church that millions of people fellowship with every day. You pay your tithes and offerings every month in cable, satellite and energy bills. The material on each channel creates a radio frequency of emotional energy that connects billons of people, so if someone extremely famous were to pass away every viewer would feel it even though they may have never physically met the person. The channels with the most influence, makes the most money.

The energy bill from the TVs being on all day and night produce multiple strings of income for multinational, corporations and companies...These international power, gas, water and light companies own multiple TV channels, making billions on both sides of the fence. The true white man owns the TV and it is a conglomerate company.

This is why the TV influences us to spend all of our money on their business partners' products. Most of the products we use and buy are products that are owned by white man whose great, great, great, great, grandparents were white slave-masters.

Television is a trillion dollar white man vision that is such a powerful marketing tool. The subliminal messaging is in the videos, the commercials, the news and the movies. The things we watch sometimes sends out messages about past, present or future events. They also send out messages about higher up knowledge or secret activities. Some programs connect to each other.

The creators of some of these TV shows get their information from associates who sometimes are the elites of the world. So the messages are sometimes hard to understand but if you really pay attention you may figure out the secret. Messages are everywhere and they connect to everything.

Today if you go to you-tube you will find many songs, movies, cartoons and TV shows secretly foretold the coming day of the World Trade Center tragedy. The Matrix told you that life is fake and computer generated. Star-Trek and Star Wars told you generations ago that there is unknown forces, spaceships, extraterrestrials and advanced technology.

The TV show Lucifer which started early 2016 tells you that the white man is the devil and the world is to picture the devil as a funny sexual good guy who works for the police. TV is an infectious force that has confused billions. This is evidence of the white man's white power.

Cartoons

Powers of the air have been working corruption in all of our minds for many years. Not only do grown-ups have to be brainwashed into receiving violent, sexual and controversial subjects in our minds from adult material, the children are also being sub consciously forced to receive this material because the same material is in their cartoons.

We are programmed to put our children through these mind control tactics as early as infancy. I remember watching pioneer cartoons. The ones that formed the cartoons of today. Mickey Mouse, Tom and Jerry, The Loony Tunes, Road Runner and Coyote, Bugs Bunny and duck season wabbit season. The cartoons that took full influence of the 21st century's children are the Simpsons, Sponge Bob, Family Guy, American Dad, South Park and Robot Chicken.

I never knew all these cartoons had hidden messages in them until I began to research, listen, and pay attention. I discovered that these cartoons have hidden messages that influences children to have sex, do drugs, kill people, use profanity, be satanic, be a homosexual or totally disrespect black people.

Some cartoons have sexual organs hidden in them and if you pay attention you might see the word sex, you might see a penis, a vagina or the number of man. We are quick to put our children in front of the TV unconscious to the fact that we are sometimes corrupting them. It's really time to cut the TV off sometime and start having more conversation and interaction with the kids. But who am I. Only a messenger.

Fake Reality TV

Reality T.V shows are leading to the destruction of the family. These characters are viewed as normal people and not actors. People don't understand that TV shows are scripted. No matter how close to real they may behave, these characters all have a script that must be followed.

Most of the reality actors whether they be black or white, share in a common character. That character is to act like a damn monkey, deceive people, act rude, act rich and tell people's business. Some of the actors in these shows have magnetic personalities, prominent careers or they're married to someone with a prominent career.

Some of these actors are pastors of churches and they too share in acting a damn fool. They act a fool and influence America to act a fool. They make it cool to cuss, snitch, act ratchet, drink and fight. This is what the evil white man wants. To destroy the entire family structure, especially black America's.

The white powered TV producers of these shows coach these reality TV stars to act aggressive, ignorant, promote wealth, vanity, sexism, show lots of emotion and argue over dumb stupid subjects which causes drinks to fly and fights to start. These actions transform the reality stars from doctors, lawyers, preachers, wives, business owners and music moguls, into ignorant uneducated thots, trap house and section 8 queens who date lazy ninjas who are unemployed. These shows gravitate to all audiences and they send a negative energy through the TV that promotes confusion, LGBT, violence and negativity.

They are even getting away with showing the same show over and over again, to hypnotize you into supporting the blatant demoralization of family life. What happened to creating scripted shows like the old school family sitcoms that show family values and how to keep a family together and not tear it apart? The programs that give your life lessons and good family laughter? Shows like Good Times, Little House on the Prairie, Sanford and Son, The Brady Bunch, The Jeffersons, All in The Family, The Cosby Show, Family Matters, Full House, A Different World, Roseanne, Living Single, Friends, and if you want to laugh just watch a little Martin. Just to name a few. Tyler Perry

These programs were not viewed as reality shows but the message in them related more to reality than the programing you are viewing nightly now. The majority of reality TV programming other than cooking, fishing and home repair shows don't provide any message or have any purpose but to teach you how to act like an ass, worship material things, destroy yourself and those who come in contact with you. This is the world's reality; turn the damn TV off!

Music

Music has the power to open up doors deep down inside of you. Doors that create energy, feeling, influence, decision making and purpose. The 3 categories of music that most affected me through my life were gospel, rhythm and blues, hip hop or should I say rap music, because to me there's no more hip hop music.

Gospel music was created to help us get through the bad times in hopes of a brighter future. Back in slave times black folk used to hum Negro spirituals to get through all the pain. Singing songs helped ease the pain and made frowns turn into smiles. I grew up in the church so church music will forever live in me. The church music today is alright but it's nothing like them old school church songs or spirituals.

Rhythm and blues came on the scene and this music also made you feel good when times were terrible. There was a lot of knowledge in the music and you could actually learn a lot about how to live and how to love. It sometimes made you wanna stand up and fight the powers that be, like the Isley Brothers and Public Enemy. Many battles were fought and fear turned into courage.

Then it was an era when rhythm and blues made you wanna meet somebody, fall in love and make a family. There was hardly ever any cussing in the music back then and it always made you wanna dance. When the slow song came on, it was time to find the girl of your dreams and ask her to dance. The best part of the slow song was the slow dance, man those were days.

Then came the hip hop era. This movement was the largest revolution of black Americans. This music was an expression of the neighborhood and it first supported the empowerment of the black race. In the beginning there was no cussing and this music also made you just wanna dance. Black folk finally had a music that the white folk didn't steal at first. Even though Blondie's Rapture rap was the first rap song on MTV. The door for black rappers on MTV came open when the pioneer rap group Run DMC and Jam Master J., collaborated on the song Walk This Way with Aerosmith.

Hip hop gave birth to new forms of dance including ticking, pop locking and breakdancing. This was the best dance era of all times. The 70's and 80's brought the babies and the 90's defined me. Rappers became the ultimate role model for people in all projects and communities in America. Then it happened, the birth of Gangster Rap.

This music was the marketing tool that became a physiological weapon. This weapon was used to create generational genocide and enslave the mind and body of the young black nation. It became the record company's largest money maker. The record company owners and executives who were deeply involved in white supremacy saw the powerful influence of this music and decided to make billions on both sides of the fence.

They corrupted the entire nation influencing gangster rap artists to promote violence, sex, weapons, gangs and drugs while funding prison construction projects and buying up a whole lot of shares. That way millions of fans listening to gangster rap music will die at a young age or be influenced to partake in criminal activity and go to prison.

Many gangster rap artists have also died at a young ages and many have went to prison. This connects the artists and the fans because they both experience brainwashing and institutional genocide from the music.

Pants sagging in prison, pants sagging on the artists, pants sagging on 1 billion fans all exposing the ass, promoting high fashion, swag and availability for sex. The music business is bigger than music. It's the business of mind control, slavery, LGBT and the destruction of the black male.

Gangster rap was the form of hip hop that was an expression of the environment and it told many true stories of street life in the majority of black communities. Fast forward a few decades now there is the trap music, bop music and flip flop music. The white artists have gone to soul and black artists have gone to pop.

The trap music is basically selling drug music. The beats hit hard and the melodies are similar to nursery rhymes. This music supports selling drugs, doing drugs, making money, partying, flossing and having a chopper. In the clubs now the dancing consist of twerking, gigging, leaning and rocking, snapping, and doing the Nae-Nae. Rap artists now wear tight pants like women and some of them even wear dresses.

Many years ago Easy E from the pioneer rap group NWA exposed one of his members of wearing the dress. The homosexual influence is in everything. Sexual expression has possessed the music so much that women have downgraded themselves into letting their breasts and buttocks just hang out. Young girls promote their bodies like new rims on old cars. Females take pictures poking their lips out and sticking their tongue out like lizards. Little girls learn twerking from their mothers and their favorite female music stars. They encourage the little girls to become strippers like them when they become adults.

The music now welcomes women to pursue careers in stripping, bartending and tricking so dressing sexy and half naked is ok. There is no more knowledge in the music and music award shows are ground 0 for the pollution of the mind by profanity, strong sexual content, violence, drug abuse, masonic symbolism and the acceptance of lesbian, gay, bisexual and transgender he/she shape shifters.

The negative influences are polluting the music right now. The power of the music business, who gives us our music has some dark origins.

It is rumored that some record companies have actually done satanic rituals invoking spirits to bless albums, to possess listeners and increase record sells. Subliminal messages are put in many records when played forwards or backwards. These messages influence the listeners to become victims or aggressors.

Music artists also become victims of this influence being offered drugs, money, sex, fortune and fame in return for a sometimes a large commitment. This commitment is rumored to sometimes be the artist's masters, soul or manhood. In the event of the artist breaking the contract or trying to save their soul, it's also rumored that death will come visit the artist in the form of an overdose or weird death. Bob Dylan almost said he sold his soul to the devil on national TV. Other recording artists have mentioned in their songs of selling their soul and some male artists have even began to start wearing dresses, skirts and skin tight pants. This is evidence of the homosexual creed which is a part of the entire New World Order.

The fans who connect with the artists are influenced to support the message and the nature of the music. The music then forms a culture, an attitude, a speech, fashion and a lifestyle. Lately the influence of music has been destroying the minds of an entire generation.

The music has corrupted a major part of the black community, which is why it's self-destructing. You must come to the realization that some of these white powered record companies are governed by power and they worship the devil and 666 is their god. Money is always first then dope. You wanna know what's wrong with all the young people? Well listen to some of the music today and you might find the answer. It's all in the music.

PART VI Two Broken Covenants

The same sex marriage act of 2013 breaks the first 2 covenants that were given to man by the Almighty God. These two covenants are the covenant of the rainbow and the covenant of the circumcision. According to scripture both of these covenants were supposed to be everlasting, meaning forever.

Read Genesis 9:16 and 17:13, these covenants are similar because they both deal with sex, sexual energy and sexual organs.

The Creator gave the first covenant to man after the judgement in the book of Genesis 9:12-15... His mighty wrath came because of the violence that was upon the face of the earth, after the sexual relations between the fallen angels and human beings in Genesis 6. These relations created offspring that were involved in violence and sexually immoral acts. Every thought of mankind became evil which led the Creator to destroy mankind with water and save the faithful Noah, his 7 family members and the animals of the earth.

The rainbow was given by God as a sign to mankind that he would never again destroy all human beings by water.

The second covenant given to man deals with the penis. The organ that makes a man a man. Throughout biblical history men were ordered to circumcise men and in many cases this led to the defeat of rival armies or other nations, because of all the pain and the lengthy healing process. The covenant in Genesis 17 made man clean unto God, by man offering a piece of the magical rod that procreates life.

The blessing to Abraham was not only to remind him that he would be the father of many nations but also that his name would have ham added. Remember his name was first Abram. Adding ham which means black, added the black race as his promised children. This is probably why black men have an enormous blessing. A common euphemism is black men have an oversized sex organ.

This explains previous racist white men making laws to prevent black men from interaction with white women and their constant curiosity of the black man's penis. The rainbow and the circumcision were the 2 covenants that were giving by God.

The last 2 of his laws in Leviticus 18:22-23, explain his extreme anger against men having sex with men and both sexes having sexual relations with animals. Currently in the 21st century both of these everlasting covenants are irrevocably broken.

The first covenant which represents the sign and symbol of the rainbow is now associated with the LGBT community. This is a violation. This also violates the 2nd covenant which deals with a man's penis because now men can marry men and women can marry women. The same sex act of 2013 confirms these 2 broken covenants and the Supreme Court acceptance in 2015 enforces the violation.

This is all part of the New World Order, the same sex acceptance and the promoting of a new LGBT society and community. There is serious negative energy that comes from same sex actions, especially from males. A male's semen is supposed to go in a female's vagina to procreate. This is the blessing from God, to be fruitful and multiply. The blessing now comes from man and they say it is okay for a man to make a man his wife or husband and plant seeds in anal areas that don't produce fruit.

These same issues is what brought the judgement back in the days of Noah and the destruction of Sodom and Gomorrah. It is an abomination in the sight of God. The promotion in the media is forcing a same sex acceptance and influence. It's in the music, the celebrities, the movies, commercials, church and in fashion.

Men are rapidly turning into women and women are turning into men. Even in comedy I find it very strange that almost every major black comedian has put on a dress, heels, make up, nails and lip stick in an attempt to advance their careers. This brought many of them fame, fortune and recognition throughout the world.

Dave Chappelle exposed the dress, letting you know that Hollywood has always been in agreement with the LGBT acceptance. He turned down a 50 million dollar contract because of his refusal of wearing the dress and promoting homosexual content.

The comedy duo Key and Peele have taken his place because they accept the dress. Their success has elevated them to gigs with the president. They have become the 2 Black Kings of comedy who wear dresses. Hollywood and comedy has always been in agreement with the LGBT homosexual acceptance for a very long time.

In the 1970's comedy roast of Richard Pryor, he jokingly said he had sex with a fag and his comedian friend who was with him was also a rumored homosexual. Hollywood and TV is in agreement with homosexuality, being a transvestite or turning into another sex. The Olympian Bruce Jenner was the precursor for it to be ok to morph or shape shift into a woman. He received a tweet from the Big Chief congratulating him her for his her courage.

The reality show I am Jazz made it ok for all children to morph into another sex. Jaden Smith reportedly wants to mutilate himself and participate into the gender shapeshifting. I would receive a mental disability check in the past if I told my mom that was a woman inside a man's body and I'm going to cut my penis off, turn it into a vagina and change my name to Davina. The federal government in 2015 says this is wonderful now. These things should not be.

Don't ask won't tell? America has come all the way out of the closet on this one. Ian Mc Kellen who played Magneto in the X-men movies announced the slogan of coming out the closet years ago. The American government is now telling it all and it is a victory and change for the evolution of America. Really it's the deviloution of America.

Now men can switch a little harder when they wear their high heels. Women can pimp a little harder when they wear their dress shoes and Michael Jordan's. This New World Order act will bring the bankrupt government new bills that will generate trillions of new tax dollars from the 50 state change. This change will also create many new careers and corporations.

The new covenant for the LGBT community is a white devil law, proving that God's will is only obeyed in Heaven. This man- made law will bring in so much confusion and the most affected will be the children. This law has led thousands to seek a petition for a new rainbow flag.

This man-made law is a law proving that the white man thinks he's God because according to the scriptures Leviticus 18:22-30 and Genesis 6:5-8, these are the same things that brought worldwide destruction and the recreation of man through Noah.

The Satanist Aleister Crowley said that the white man would do what thou wilt and it would be the law. The white man is the god of this earth and he used a black man to bring in a sexually immoral white devil law. Obama announced the acceptance of the Supreme Court ruling in favor of men and women being transgender. In my opinion he didn't appear or sound sincere.

The devil influences all positions in power. It doesn't matter what color skin he or she represents. The white devil power is blood money, power, control, deception, slavery, murder, child molestation and having anal sex. These man made laws curse God to His face and fuels the judgement of fire to become hotter than hot.

These violations don't mean that there won't be curses of water. God promised not to destroy all flesh but you best believe that some flesh will be destroyed. The tsunamis, the typhoons, the tornados, the hurricanes, the rain storms, the floods, the snow storms, the earthquakes and the murders around the world confirm the two broken covenants. So think it not strange the fiery trials and tribulations of destructive natural phenomena to come pay a visit every now and then.

It's just part of God's judgement and signs of the times. There will be more judgements especially after the recorded earth day of June 26 2015, the day of the two broken covenants.

PART VII Black Truth about Christianity

Christianity is the good ole American religion. Most Americans are Christians and when you're a Christian in America you're considered a good or righteous person. You may be a model citizen, college educated, church going and you have a great job and Oh you're a Christian! You're such a great person now. This is really how the general public thinks.

If you think this way about Christians, excuse my English but you are stupid. Just because you say you're a Christian doesn't mean you're a Christian. You can say you're a Christian but really be a devil. I grew up in the church so I know a few devils who swear that they're Christians.

I'm a descendant of ministers and musicians so when I was a child, I was forced by family law to go to church at least 4 times out of the week. My mom has always been a lead minister of music so I had to attend all choir rehearsals. Bible study, Sunday school, Sunday service, afternoon service, gospel concerts, vacation Bible school, revivals, conventions, and I loved those times. They were great! I grew up so fast and when situations forced me to slow down and be still, I began to study science, physics, sociology, history, economics, religion and many things about Christianity.

The things that I discovered brought me to the understanding that Christianity is a copy of former religions. Religions that were African! The scriptures in the Bible that quote the 3rd Heaven, the coming of the Son of Man with thousands of angels and the translation of Enoch come from ancient Ethiopian texts.

All of the basic stories of Christianity like Christ being the Son of God come from ancient Africa. The Christian cross is a copy of the Egyptian cross the Ankh, which is the symbol for life. Jesus's burial preparation and mummification comes from methods of Egyptian Pharaohs. Even the Mother Mary holding Baby Jesus come from the African Kemetic texts. The Christian trinity also comes from ancient Africa. The father was Osiris, the mother was Isis and the Son of God was Horus, who had the all Seeing Eye. The prayers were sent up to the God Amen-Ra. Christians, Judaists and Muslims say Amen after every prayer unconscious to the fact that saying Amen is promoting Africa in every breath. This is the Black Truth about Christianity.

Christianity is supposed to be modeled after the Messiah Jesus Christ but I found that the doctrines, laws and ordinances that Jesus taught, are totally opposite of what the religion Christianity teaches. Anything that is half true is not of God. Anything that is a quarter of the truth still is not God and anything that is even a tenth of the truth is not God. Falsehood and half-truths are attributes of Satan, not God.

All Christian denominations including Jehovah Witness were created by the white man. The 16th century was when the Baptist denomination was created and black people were getting hung, raped and murdered during this time. There are too many Christian denominations to name but they all originate from the mother domination which is the Latin Roman Catholics. The Roman Empire is the only institution in the world that is operating today in our day and age as it was in the days of Jesus Christ. Shall I remind you that priests and the governor of the Roman Empire crucified Christ and let a murderer go free? Shall I remind you that Roman priests, presidents, governors and slave masters of America, used Christianity as a physiological weapon to brainwash all races into worshiping their white God and white Jesus?

Christian laws and doctrines come from previous white god doctrines like Serapis Christus. He was Christ before Jesus Christ. The man who made himself Serapis was Ptolemy who was the 1st white pharaoh of Black Egypt.

Ptolemy was the Greek general under Alexander the Great who invaded Egypt and made himself pharaoh and god by force. This doctrine and others where integrated into Christianity during the councils of Nicaea, Laodicea and Trent. These councils of Constantine changed the laws of God and Jesus Christ, into laws of the church, Mother Mary and the Pope.

Today people go to church and believe whatever the preacher says, whatever their mother says, hardly ever what Jesus in the Bible preached. So now I'm going to show you if you have your Bible near, that the laws and doctrines that have been taught are all wrong. Since the Roman Catholic Church is the head of this Christian conspiracy, let's start there with their Holy Catholic Creed. This creed consist of 3 main beliefs:

The first one is the infallibility of the Pope.

The second is the Immaculate Conception.

The third is the ascension of Mother Mary immediately after her death.

The first order of the creed already shows resemblance of a satanic order. I say this because there is no mention of God the Father. This order not only denies God but sets up a man as God by saying that he cannot fail. God is the only one who never fails and there is none beside Him. According to this order the Pope's word never fails. This totally violates the first commandment and the following three commandments which are unto God.

In all things we are to first acknowledge God and give him praise. The most important prayer that Jesus taught us to pray begins with 'Our Father'. The first order of the Catholic Church first gives honor to the Pope? Even in the Quran, every scripture first gives honor to God who is most gracious and most merciful.

We are not supposed to first give honor to man or woman, these are not the laws of God. These are laws of falsehood and falsehood is of the devil, so therefore the Immaculate Conception and accession of Mary may also be falsehood. Together we will let the Bible interpret the most common 7 Christian theories that you know. The Bible will show you the exact violations in interpretation.

1 The Trinity Constantine, the first Roman emperor to convert to Christianity was the precursor for the current trinity doctrine. After the Roman invasion of Africa, this doctrine was brought in during one of the monumental council meetings from a minister from Alexandria Egypt. I hold total respect unto God the Father, Jesus Christ the Son and God's Holy Spirit but there were Sumerian trinities, Reptilian trinities, Yoruba trinities, Babylonian trinities and Egyptian trinities.

Some of these were thousands of years before Christianity. There are other trinities which include Roman and Greek trinities, the freemason trinity, and the satanic trinity which consists of the beast, the reptilian dragon and the false prophet.

The trinity doctrine was integrated into Christianity just like other pagan doctrines, rituals and holidays. This was done to increase the money and the power of the Roman Catholic Church. The word trinity is not mentioned anywhere in the Bible scriptures.

God is not a trinity consisting of the Father, Son and Holy Spirit. God is not a duo consisting of God and Jesus Christ. God is one. He is God and God alone. God is one Force all by Himself. Jesus even said God is one. Read Mark 12:29-34 and listen to Jesus in the Bible and don't just keep listening to your pastor. Read and understand the word for yourself.

2 JESUS IS God Millions of Christians say Jesus is God but if you read the entire chapter of John 5, you will find that Jesus never wanted to be lifted up as being equal to God. He said his words are not his, his authority is not his, the miracles he performs are not his and he said he can do nothing without the aid from his Father!

All of these gifts were taught and given to Jesus by God. Jesus is the Heavenly prophet, teacher, messenger, messiah and savior who came down to earth with the word from God. God is God all by Himself and there is no God beside Him. Read Isaiah 40:25, 42:8, 43:11-13, 44:6 8 24, 45:5 18 21 and 46:9...God is greater than all and He gives us the opportunity to become one with Him in the spirit.

The oneness of the Spirit of Truth resides in those who obey the voice of God and his Son Jesus Christ, which Jesus explains in John 10:25-30 and in John 17: 21-23. Just because Jesus is one with God doesn't mean he is God.

He would never say he is God! He never even said he was the Son of God and corrected people when they called him the Son of God. He is the Son of man which is what he called himself. Jesus never ever called himself God in the Bible but millions call him God, blind to the fact that Christianity is a monotheistic religion. That means one God!

Jesus is the personification of a hero and every hero is subject to his master. If it is written in 1st Corinthians 15:20-28 that Jesus bows down to God, than how can Jesus be God? God Is God!

3 CALLING man FATHER Thousands of people go and confess their sins to a catholic priest that they call father. Besides your earthly father or someone that takes care of you like a father, you by the law of Jesus Christ are to call no man father. You are not to even call Jesus father.

In Mathew 23:8-12, Jesus says you only have one Father who is God the Father and one Rabbi/Teacher who is Jesus Christ but don't listen to me or Jesus in the Bible, just keep calling your catholic priest father.

4 Resurrection Day Sunday resurrection is another twisted theory and tradition orchestrated by the Roman Catholic Church. So many preachers preach the sermon of Jesus dying on Good Friday and then raising up from the dead early Sunday morning. This sermon is mostly preached during the holiday of Easter and after church people go on Easter egg hunts, eat chocolate bunny rabbits and give out Easter egg baskets. Do you not see the contradictions with this holiday?

This holiday praises Jesus, eggs, candy and a bunny rabbit at the same time. Now comes the truth behind the white lie.

Jesus said that he must suffer and be put to death and spend 3 days and 3 nights in the heart of earth. He explains this as the sign of Jonah in Matthew 12:40 However you look at it 3 days equals 72 hours. Not 56 hours nor 48. If Jesus was placed in the tomb on Friday at 3, 4, 5,6,7,8 or 9 o'clock pm, 72 hours from any one of these times would mean he rose from the grave on Monday, the day of the moon!

If you know how to add and if you're at least 7 years old, you would be able to figure this out. The Sunday resurrection arithmetic is off. The sequence of events leading to the death and resurrection of Christ failed to calculate the obedience to the Sabbaths, the Passover and the Feast of Unleavened Bread. These feasts begin on the 14th and 15th on Wednesday or Thursday, read Leviticus 23:5-6 The Messiah's faithful female servant arrived at the tomb on the first day of the week and Jesus was already risen from the grave!

The 7 day Sabbath ends Saturday at sunset which is probably around the time that he rose from the grave. Keep listening to your pastor when he says he got up on Sunday even though facts support, that this is another white lie to praise the early rising sun.

5 The New Law Jerimiah 31:31 and Hebrews 8:8 speak of God putting the new law in our minds and writing it on our hearts. This new law does not mean that the old law doesn't apply anymore. This new covenant means that by the blood of Christ and his human sacrifice, we are to remember the law and hold on to the law. This is why this scripture is in the Old and the New Testament.

Jesus Christ is the direct intercession of God's grace. The new law that was given to mankind was nothing more than the old law manifested in the flesh of Christ.

In Mathew 5:17-20, Jesus said not one letter should pass away from the law and anyone that teaches you this will be last in the kingdom of Heaven. Jesus then tells us that the only way to enter in the kingdom is to be more righteous than the scribes and Pharisees, the same people that teach us everything.

Jesus came to fulfill and bring full meaning of the law even though millions of Christians say that they're not under the old law. My question is if you're not under God's law, then whose law are you under?

6 JOHN 3:16 So many people are going to burn in hell thinking this scripture will get them directly into Heaven. Do you know that even the devil and his demons believe in Jesus and can recite this scripture better than you and in different languages?

The church leaders who taught all of these doctrines are the ones who Jesus is talking about in Mathew 15:7-9 and Mark 7:6-7, their mouths honor Jesus but their heart is far from him therefore their worship is in vain. They teach doctrines and commandments of men violating all the commandments but mainly the first four that honor and respect God.

God so loved the world and He loved his human children so much that He gave us Jesus. He gave us Jesus to save us from the world. We are not supposed to love the world. God did that and we can't do what He did for us.

James 4:4 tells us that the world is an enemy so you have to do more than just believe in Jesus. You have to know him, follow him, learn to walk and stay on the right path with him. God loved the world and gave us Jesus because the world is polluted by the devil.

The final one totally violates the 4th commandment of the 10 commandments

7 THE SABBATH DAY The book of Daniel tells the story of the coming of the end of the world and the revolutions of ancient kingdoms and one of them is still here today. The kings of these kingdoms spoke against the Most High God. One of the kings will think to change times and laws that were given by God, another one will think he is God and one would be a homosexual.

This biblical information is evidence of the connection of the Roman Catholic Church, Kings, Queens, Presidents, the government, white Jesus, white slave masters, the homosexual influence, and the changes that they make to the laws, the Ten Commandments and the changing of the Sabbath day.

The Sabbath day was changed from Saturday to Sunday, a day that praised the sun god Mithra and other pagan gods. Pagan god holidays were changed to holidays that pay homage to Jesus and praises to the seasons when they change. The Roman winter solstice connects this sun worship to Jesus. He is referenced as being The Sun of Righteousness in the bible verse Malachi 4:2.

The seasonal change in December brought the holiday Christmas. Reference to December 25th being the birthday of Jesus is not mentioned anywhere in the Bible scriptures! We just hold on to the tradition and ignore the Bible when it comes to Christmas and what date and day he was born. Christmas is yet another white lie confirming that the white man is the devil. Now pay attention.

All of these holidays except one is Happy! Happy Presidents day, Happy Labor day, Happy 4th, Happy Mother's day, Happy Father's day, Happy Easter, Happy Thanksgiving and Happy New Year. I mean every holiday is Happy, even the day designated as the devil's day is happy, Happy Halloween. Your birthday which is really your New Year is also prefaced with the word happy.

Every store, church, bank, man, woman, child, white, black, brown, red, yellow, person in the world is Happy during holidays! The entire nation is Happy. Pharrell Williams is Happy. So think about it.

Every holiday you celebrate you are Happy including your soul day but when you celebrate Christmas you say Merry Christmas? On this day you are merry? Not happy? Are you merry? Everybody is merry? I mean like Merry Birthday and Merry New Year?

Who in the 21st century really talks like this in America? Nobody! Why don't we say Happy Christ's Day and why is the Mas on the end of Christ and not day? Are you listening? Pay Attention!

When you say Merry Christmas you're really saying a Roman Catholic trinity consisting of <u>Mary</u>, <u>Christ</u> and Catholic <u>Mass</u>. This supports the Roman Catholic Church and first gives praise to Mother Mary, Jesus Christ and finally Catholic Mass.

Then on top of all of this confusion, the world's tradition is to also praise a fat old white man who has the power to give you what you ask. This man is not God, this man was St. Nicholas a Roman minister who probably owned slaves. The white man transformed him into a white pagan god who really is a white devil. The letters in his name can even spell out Satan/Santa.

Songs are sung to this white man, parents and teachers tell children he's watching and he knows everything. Christmas is a holiday tradition to tell white lies and sing praise to a fat old white man, Mary, baby Jesus and Catholic mass. This is hypocrisy.

There are three Christmas songs that tell the universal truths about Christmas and how people feel at Christmas time.

1. The song by the Emotions, What Do the Lonely Do, tells a very sad Christmas story because so many people are sad, lonely and hurt at Christmas that they wish it would leave and never return.

2. The song by Luther Vandross, Every Year at Christmas Time, tells a very happy Christmas story because so many sad people are smiling, being happy again at Christmas Time. They wish it could be Christmas everyday.

3. The song by Stevie Wonder, Someday Day at Christmas, is probably one of the most educating songs ever written because it tells a totally different Christmas story.

This song will make you cry if you really pay attention because his song is our white man's world reality. It's about their lives, their power, their wars, their bombs, their world, their hatred towards us, our hatred towards them, our starvation, our slavery, our dreams of freedom and our deaths.

This influences us to hope for a new world of equality, peace and freedom that may come to be, not in our times but some day at Christmas time in 2095 or 2216. Young Stevie knew in 1966 the era of the Civil Rights Movement that Christmas is a myth and people have to bend reality and accept a fake birthday for the sake of family, friends, laughter, freedom, unity, good food, music, drinks, smoke, smiles, cries, peace, love and happiness.

This day is the birthday of many previous deities that connect to the fertility god Yule, the tree god. You know yule tide carols, the green tree, the mistletoe? Yule is the female that makes love to the mistletoe. This is why when you get your head under one you can steal a kiss.

This stealing a kiss comes from European mythology and an English tradition, depicting the mistletoe as a love god with male energy. The mistletoe is a male green plant that sticks to other plants and trees and steals their water and nutrients. The male god the Mistletoe sticks to Yule the white goddess to produce the Sun at December 25th. The Christmas tree, the wreath and the mistletoe represent Yule.

In past times people and children were having sex unto Yule, some were raped unto Yule and some were sacrificed unto Yule. People's head's and body parts were dismembered, set on fire and hung on these previous tree gods but now its lights and ornaments to represent the sun, the moon and the stars. The book of Jerimiah10: 1- 16 talks about those who worship fake gods and follow the ways of heathens. God tells us not to practice the customs of other nations and this verse also speaks that cutting and fixing up a tree is in vain.

Trees and plants are very important, so much that they are looked at as physical gods. It is true that without green trees, life on earth would be extremely hard but the real worship of the green tree is due to its worldwide construction and its production of medicines and poisons. The influence of the green tree has some biblical origins.

In the beginning of the Bible in the book of Genesis 30:14-16, you will discover that the not so attractive sister Leah purchased her husband Jacob from her more attractive sister Rachel. She purchased him with green mandrake plants for sex in the field. In the Songs of Solemn 7:10-13, the beautiful black Shulamite woman was told by the King to get up early in the morning and go to the field, where the mandrakes give off their powerful smell. Then they made love. The green tree is fertility and when you have some green trees in this day and age you can receive sex for the green tree, you can make money off of the green tree, the green tree looks and smells good and if you would so happen to set it on fire.

Holidays are nothing more than white power economic franchises for the church and state. These things deny the true God and invites the church leaders to participate in making enormous profits from the enterprise of the mega church monopoly. All of these things curse God to his face. The leaders have allowed Satan to pollute the temples of God.

If you read the entire chapters of Ezekiel 8-9, you will read that the satanic god named jealously was standing in the entrance of the temple of God. This was making God very jealous and very angry. The priestly elders of the temple were inside with their backs turned on God facing and worshipping the sun and other mammal and reptilian gods. Judgment came upon the priest and upon all of the men, women, and children that supported this satanic worship.

They were sentenced to death and their bodies were piled up in the church to defile it. Those who did not support this worship were marked and saved because God's law was in their minds and in their hearts.

His Law needs to be in our hearts. We need to worship God in spirit and in truth and not let people who are not about the right tell us how to carry our cross. Because the cross that there carrying just might be the one that's upside down.

I have 2 additional points I would like to make. The first one is about the corruption of Christianity on TV.

Some of the pastors and preachers that preach on these broadcasting networks are wonderful and God bless all of you who are not using the word to deceive and make enormous profits, these are the true followers of God and Jesus Christ. But to the ones who are corrupt, I call them the DDD's, Digital Devil Dealers.

Most of these televangelist live lavish lifestyles and always preach prosperity. They have enormous churches that make millions of dollars every week in tithes and offerings. These pastors constantly influence and encourage millions of church members and viewers to send in seed money. These pastors do fake healings, employ staff to assist in the fake healings, employ people to lie about the fake healings and employ people to lie about seed gifts. These people claim to have been healed and some claim that they received money gifts like 40 thousand, another 100 thousand, even a million dollar money shower!

Then after all the pastor's good preaching, reading, the Bible, praying, singing, shouting, crying and lying by putting it all in the name of Jesus, the pastor has the nerve to ask his viewers for 5 thousand dollars in seed money. Tell me what kind of representative of God does fake healings, steals millions of dollars everyday and encourages people to lie? These preachers and pastors are spreading anti-Christianity destroying the spiritual mind and the true knowledge God. These preachers and pastors are black and white and they are devils! This the Black Truth.

The other point I would like to make about Christianity is in Matthew 5:44, this is one of the main scriptures that is preached by preachers and politicians. This particular scripture is one that separates Christianity from other religions. Some Christians really believe that they're supposed to love their enemies like they love their brothers and sisters.

Fools! You are supposed to love your enemies from a distance! I personally have forgiven many of my enemies but I would never give them a glass of water or a piece of bread. I forgiving them is blessing them enough because I truthfully desire to kill a few of them but I won't for the sake of Matthew 5:44

How can you love and bless the devil who is your chief enemy? The people who have wronged you, the ones who hate and despise you and those who are jealous of you are the people who are riding with the devil. They desire to see you fail. How can you love your enemies that want to kill, steal and destroy you and your family? How can you love your enemies who want to have sex with your 3 and 4 year old children? How can you love enemies like that?

These things are preached and taught by preachers and politicians to keep you spiritually blind and keep you turning the other cheek. These things allow your enemies to keep stealing from you so you continue to be brainwashed and enslaved. Stop being immature listening and believing white lies.

God destroys his enemies and he does not love them! Read Psalm 5:6, Psalm 68:21, Psalm 143:12, Psalm 109, Isaiah27:1. You cannot love God who is your friend and love the devil who is your enemy!

This does not make any sense. You have to love one and hate the other. Life is a war and in battle you destroy your enemies, not bless them nor support them. I hate the enemy! I will never love him. If I find that one of my friends has transformed into the enemy, I would hate him as well.

There is enmity between me and the enemy and God said so in Genesis 3:15. Enmity means hostility! Minister Malcom X said it best. He stated that an eye for an eye is a good religion! A hand for a hand, a foot for a foot, a head for a head, that's a good religion! This is secretly the true religion of man.

Your enemies are blessed if you allow them to live. Your enemies are like rats, roaches and flies inside your house. They will take over your house if you let them so you must get weapons that utterly destroy them. If you have enemies and you don't desire to end their lives, than you're extremely brainwashed and must not be a real Christian, Muslim, American or human.

If your enemies murdered everybody in your family except you and then told you to worship their flag, their Jesus and their God, should you? Hell no! Unfortunately this is what has been going on for years, blessing the enemy. Believe what you want about loving your enemies but to all the diehard Christians and to the all the citizens tell me this;

Did King David bless Goliath the enemy? Or did he cut his enemy's head off and drag it through the king's palace? Did British/ America bless their Asian Japanese enemies in 1945? Or did they drop 2 atomic nuclear bombs within 72 hours that killed 100 thousands of Asian men, women and children. Open up your eyes.

White Jesus

Everybody knows that American Christians predominately believe in a full blooded Aryan looking white Jesus with blond hair and blue eyes. If you think about the regions that the Bible says Jesus was born, where he grew up, where God called him and where he preached, you would be stupid to believe this.

This white Jesus thing started a long time ago under the domination of the Roman Catholic Church. The great artist Michael Angelo painted Caucasian descriptions of Christ and other biblical heroes. They were accepted by the Roman Catholic Church and the rest is history. Later in time the artist Warner Salman created the "Head of Christ" image which became America's poster child Jesus.

This white Jesus image has been reproduced over a half a billion times and depicts the blond hair blue eye Jesus, which came around the same time as Hitler's blond haired blue-eyed Aryan in the 1940's. This increased the influence of the white man Jesus theory and brainwashed all white, black, brown, red and yellow Americans into believing in their Hitler style Jesus, who may have been born in Germany or grew up in some other European region. Certainly not the Jesus in your Bible who was born in Asia and grew up in Africa.

Understand that some of the Catholic Church leaders were devil worshipers, white racists, homosexuals, alcoholics, pedophiles, drug addicts and refused to accept the black Negro, who also was born and grew up in Africa/Asia just like Jesus. They told white lies and said that the black man was not human and Jesus was white.

Since they lied to us and told us we were not human, then the white Jesus theory must also be a lie. I'm not trying to say that Jesus is black because remember, a black man is an African American. Jesus sure was treated exactly like an African American or should I say he was treated like a nigger. Let us recall the scene:

He was falsely accused and tormented by his own people. He was snitched on and sold out by his so called friend. The priest and the legislature brought charges against him with laws that were created by his Father. He was arrested by racist white police, he was spit on, beat, cursed out, humiliated, whipped, mutilated, stripped butt naked, stabbed and on top of all this the Roman governor let a convicted murderer go free in return to crucify the Lord and sweet Jesus forgave them. Those deceitful white devils! If this isn't evidence of the connection of Jesus and the black man I don't know what is.

The white man of the past said that black folk were kind, full of love and forgiveness just like Jesus. They told the black man that God didn't create them and that they didn't have a soul. They said that God made them to be slaves to the white man forever and they constantly said that God was white and Jesus was white.

The black-men were cursed and talked about because of their wooly hair and thick lips but if you turn your Bible to Daniel 7:9 it reads: "I beheld till the thrones were cast down and the Ancient of days did sit, whose garment was white as snow and the hair of his head like pure wool, his throne like the fiery flame and his wheels as burning fire".
Revelation 1:14 says: "His head and his hairs were white like wool, as white as snow and his eyes were as a flame of fire". The Bible says the Father and the Son have hair like wool, just like African/Asian men but the white man promotes the Father and Son with straight hair like the European man, totally opposite of the Bible.

This proves that the white Jesus description is yet another white lie created by the white man and according to the 1st 4 commandments, we are not supposed to bow down to an idol not even white Jesus idols. There are white Jesus idols spread out across the world. The white man has corrupted the true meaning of Christ, which is why lightning has struck some of these white Jesus statues. The Christ the Redeemer Statue in Brazil was struck by lightning breaking the right thumb. The King of Kings Statue in Ohio was also struck by lightning in the right hand but this one burnt to the ground. Jesus being the right hand of God, is probably the reason the right hand of white Jesus statues have been struck by lightning. This phenomenon is an act of God and is meant to awaking you to remember the first 4 commandants.

According to scripture we are to bow down to no other gods, or make graven images and idols but if you look around that's what a lot of people have been doing. Bowing down to white Jesus statues means you don't care about the first 4 commandments.

If Jesus appeared on earth in the American black slavery times he would be persecuted just like the black people were. He still was persecuted and the institution of the Roman Government who governed and participated in killing Jesus, is the same institution who is governing in this day and age. They are called Roman Christians and their Pope has bowed down to a Black Mary and a Black Jesus in Spain and in other regions. This is the Black Truth.

PART VIII Intelligent Designer

Throughout my intense studies I found that the origin of humanity and every animate and inanimate thing on the face of the earth, came forth from a thought. Every piece of matter, every atom, electron, proton, neutron, mineral, element, DNA cell, microorganism, amino acid, came from an electromagnetic super symmetric thought.

The existence of life, energy, space, and time, mass, the order and laws of all things began with the Intelligent Designer's thought. The design that he thought about came before the beginning of the galaxy and universe. Understand that this was done in and out of time like Maya Angelou would say.

The Creator is not bound by time or space, so the human mind would never know exactly how and when this all happened. The galaxy, universe and the solar energy that proceeded from the Designer's thought had to have hit speeds faster than light and hotter than fire. Mind you that this thought may have been as small as one grain of sand or salt or even smaller! The creation was obedient to the thought and in came the lightning spark that ignited the energies that made the subatomic nuclear, intergalactic explosion. Bang, bang, boom, boom, this was the Big Bang!

The solar energies and the positive forces of nature compel the force of dark energy. The natural, electromagnetic, gravitational and nuclear forces are balanced by an anti-gravitational weak force, so that the power of nothing is the beginning of something. The nuclear induced gasses and dust came and assisted with the thought of stars, planets, moons and the suns. The spark of creation still resides in the inner core of most planets, so the intense heat and fire will never cool. The will of the thought is obeyed. The inner core of earth has been on fire for how long now?

Other planets have other species that have been created with higher intelligence and other physical forms. These beings are foreign to the dominate human being of the earth. Some of these beings of the Heavens and the planets obey the law and order of the Creator. These would be the Holy Angels, Holy Watchers, Good Aliens and Good Humans. Some of the beings of the Heavens and planets do not obey the law and order of the Creator and fell out of sync with the Creator. These would be the fallen angels, demons, devils, evil aliens and evil humans.

In the beginning when plants, animals and humans were first created, water surrounded the outside of the earth and came up out of the ground from the inside of the earth. In these times water and the magical gas oxygen was in abundance. The earth is a living organism and water and oxygen create life. Inhaling so much of this pure life giving element would make every creation back then extremely large, including plant life and animal life.

Other beings from other places often visited the creation and monitored the process. Those who fell from their higher up level begin to intercede with the human race and giants became the offspring of the intercession. Many fossils of giant reptilian creatures have been found confirming a visitation of a reptilian race. There has also been fossils that have been found of giant human like mammals, confirming a time of the giant humans that once dominated the face of the earth.

The history books say that the human being came from the ape and then evolved to the Australopithecines of Africa, where Mrs. Ples and Mrs. Lucy were found. They then migrated to Europe and turned white and were called the Neanderthals. Later on they were called the Homosapien and eventually turned into Homosexuals.

The Austral –Hetero-Homo Formula

God– Earth-Africa--Australpelethicins-He-tero-sexual=1 bloodline offspring

God-Earth-Africa-Europe-Ho-mosapinas-Ho-mo-sexual=0 bloodline offspring

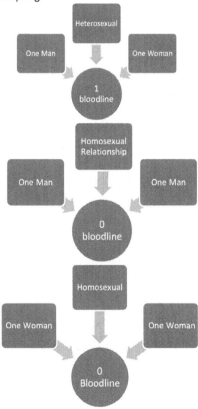

The creation has been disputing with the Creator for a very long time and we all know this brings judgement. The biblical account of Noah speaks of the flood that wiped out mostly all life on the planet earth and then the Creator repopulated it. Corruption, confusion and violence continue to fill the earth and it has grown to a size that is almost equal to the times of the flood.

What does the future hold? Is the next step to our evolution extinction? The predictions of the Mayans scared a lot of people but you still have to remember the predictions that are in the Bible and Quran. Also Socrates, Herodotus, Aristotle, Nostradamus even todays NASA. They all speak of a future catastrophic event that has never been. The super scientist of the 21st century are attempting to copy the Intelligent Designer's Divine thought with the CERN creation of the Large Hadron Collider.

This machine has the power to collide particles at the speed of light and generate trillions of degrees of heat. This man made power can generate the luminosity and temperature of a star. They are trying to recreate the energy and the electromagnetic power of the divine thought and open up portals to other dimensions. This may be why all the weather is out of whack.

The god like scientists know that there is possibility of a future event that will bring a nuclear and bio chemical catastrophe, which will rain fire and globally infect every part of the earth. Shouldn't you prepare? Shouldn't you make sure that you and your family are in sync and rotation with the Creator? Or should you just not listen and not pay attention to the Divine Thought.

"God bless our children for they are under attack!"

Evolution, School, and the Outcome.

The American school system has an agenda that goes back like a few hundred years. Not only do our children have to learn and believe everything that the teacher teaches, they are forced to learn doctrines that contradict the theory of creation and its process.

Creation was once taught in schools but with the power of white power, evolution overthrew God in public schools.

The evolution theory is really a white man religion that was founded by Charles Darwin. This theory became popular around the same time that black folk were being recognized during the Reconstruction era. Evolution paved a way for an entirely new scientific way to look at life. This theory basically says that all life is a chance of random processes and that cells mutate and change by themselves, over a period of time. My question is why haven't we grew wings?

This ideology also says that there is a natural selection of survival like the reptile. Kill or be killed, a dog eat dog world, big bank take little bank, I eat you starve.

Evolution = there is no Intelligent Designer, the world created itself over longs periods of time, humans came from animals and killing weak people is the way of life. I believe Mr. Darwin knew in his heart that something or maybe even someone created the entire design of bio chemical life, which is why he wrote The

Origin of Species which discredits his own evolutionary theory.

One cell is too remarkable to deny a supernatural, mathematician, chemist and physicist that may have created the human DNA cell. 1 DNA cell contains the design of 206 bones, 16 thousand muscles, 200 thousand genes, 2 million optic nerves, 1 billion nerve cells, 130 billion meter long veins, over 20 trillion cells. The human body is a flesh form program that has bits and codes of information in its DNA.

The body is somewhat of a wireless biochemical machine, which has the similarities of an electronic computerized robot with physical upgrades of memory, emotions and consciousness. Your brain is the computer and video recorder. Your body, skin and bones is the metal frame. Your heart is the engine that pumps the electric blood. Your red, blue and green veins are the wires that conduct the liquid electricity. Water and food is your fuel for energy. Your spirit force is your battery. You must understand that you are an electromagnetic element that entered into a bio-chemical white man matrix at birth. The matrix is 6 electrons, 6 protons, 6 neutrons, 666. You have a time limit and when your time expires you exit out of the matrix.

You have the same ingredients in you that are in stars, minerals, rocks, soil, water, plants and animals. You even have electricity in you. Your brain travels faster than the speed of light and its activity is very similar to the stars in the universe and the World Wide Web. It connects to billions of pieces of information, just as stars connect to planets, suns and dimensions. There is a 1 percent enhancement in our DNA that separates us from the design of the chimpanzee. This 1 percent is a conscious force of intelligence, technology, communication and super information.

This human DNA enhancement had to have come from out of space, which would explain the revolutionary inventions of many intelligent men. (Cars, planes, jets, weapons, radios, TV's, phones, computers, robotics, etc.) These intelligent men discovered information from space that already existed in the past. This answers the question of an Intelligent Designer. The information in space is downgraded into the creation over a period of time. Trees, fruits, animals, humans, stars, earth, wind, fire, water, are different designs that have not been created by the white man but the white man will tell you that atoms produce designs and programs by themselves. It is entirely impossible for designs and processes to take place, without the aid of some type of super powerful energy force.

The problem with Evolution is it never explains how the chance of processes began. Time did not exist when the Big Bang happened nor did humans. So can this theory be taken as the truth? The only thing that Evolution does is deny the possibility of a super intelligent being that has divine consciousness, who has the blueprints, codes and equations of all creations. All designs have a Designer and all programs have a Programmer!

The Evolution theory started early in the history of the school system, along with a group of programs that secretly brainwashed children. One was called OBE, Outcome Based Education, which monitors the entire life of a student who's taught these different subjects and programs. The NEA, National Education Association and the NCA, National Councils of Education, had no use for the supernatural or God and sought to take biblical teaching out of public schools. Humanism, socialism and sexism was taught by teachers and the outcome is terrible.

The program called SIECUS, Sex Information and Education Council, allowed masturbation, sex and homosexuality to enter children's minds as early as kindergarten. This program allowed teachers to participate in immoral communication with students. During the Civil Rights year of 1964, Mary Calderone a medical director of Planned Parenthood became co-founder of SIECUS. She participated in a study where she witnessed a homosexual couple sodomizing each other and she said that she was "walking on air." Planned Parenthood is responsible for millions of murders by abortion, which is the number 1 killer of African Americans. They also have members that have been accused of selling fetus material.

Then came Project 10, which counsels children that believe they're homosexuals. I find it strange that there was a popular LGBT nightclub in Indianapolis Indiana called the 10. I wonder if they discovered the ideal of their name from the public school program Project 10.

In 1993, WNBC-TV in New York reported that teachers that belonged to a group called NAMBLA, North American Man Boy Love Association, were having sex with students. These are just some of the things that have happened in the past when it comes to the public evolution school system. Black children have received the worst treatment from the white American school system. They suffered brainwashing, humiliation and corruption at the hands of school officials.

White America of the past told blacks that they weren't supposed to learn and some were tortured for just trying to learn how to read and write. Now the school system doesn't encourage them to learn anything. Most young black folk these days won't even pick up a book. After the Reconstruction era, black folk finally were allowed to learn and attend schools that were semi segregated. I say this because the racist Jim Crow laws were posted on the school bulletin board. The racists' bastards posted their sin for all to see and join the dehumanization of the black man.

The first seven Jim Crow Laws

1. A black male is not to offer his hand to shake with a white male because it implies being socially equal.
2. A black male is not to offer his hand or any other part of his body to a white women because he risks being charged with rape.
3. Under no circumstance is a black male to offer a light to a white woman's cigarette
4. Blacks are not allowed to show affection to one another in public especially kissing because it offends the whites
5. Blacks are introduced to whites never whites to blacks
6. Whites do not use courtesy titles of respect towards the blacks like Mr. Mrs. Miss Sir or Ma'am blacks are to be called by their first names only
7. If a black person rides in the car with a white person he is to sit in the back seat because white motorist have the right of way at all intersections

The second 7 Jim Crow Laws

1. Never assume that a white person is lying so even a lie is the truth this probably was the creation of a white lie
2. Never impute dishonorable intentions to a white person
3. Never suggest that a white person is from an inferior class
4. Never lay claim or demonstrate any superior knowledge or intelligence in other words if you are intelligent you are supposed to act dumb
5. Never curse a white person
6. Never laugh at a white person
7. Never comment on the appearance of a white women.

Can you imagine being black going to school having to deal with such aggressive racism? The effects of the past reflect on the future because right now schools have terrible dropout rates, low test scores, confused and abused children, sex cases between teachers and students, gun and drug possessions, murders, terrorist threats, lack of funding and this is what came out of the outcome based white American school system.

PART VIIII World's Biggest Gangs
The Criminal System

The American criminal justice system was created to make enormous profits off of charging a person's body, as one would place charges on a credit card. This trillion dollar business transforms a human being into a profitable number. Once a person is arrested his body turns into an expensive bond and a material commodity. Let me explain:

You are not totally free and the law is all pro-say in codes and contracts. Your life is your name and signature and it's very powerful. It's actually more powerful than your voice and your body. The power of paper and pen or any digital signature, binds your entire being to the words in a contract. Once the signature is on paper you become an owner of property or property of the owner. If you ever were to enter into the criminal justice system the Federal Government can resign your signature on many documents. Your criminal arrest is your default judgement and you must pay. Your detainment creates credit and debt in the system. Your body is the credit and you are in the red so this helps create the debt.

This fictitious debt must be paid so the political entrepreneurs figure out how to force you and the tax payer to help pay all the bills for the buildings and all of the salaries of the many careers in the criminal justice system. The fictitious court system and the fictitious law allows them to sue you because you are in penalty for appearing as a defendant in their white slave-master court system.

If you transcend to the prison system, you create more debt that helps creates trillions for the government. The corporations are privatized and the system connects to other institutions. They make profit by housing humans like farm animals and investing in the shares of prison real estate projects. They feed the housed humans food that is not suitable for human consumption. These corporations fund the government and create the system.

The DTC, Depository Trust Corporation, and CUSIP, Committee of Uniform Information Process, have trillion dollars a day that goes through the system. They use a 6 digit number that's CUSIP International Number System. When they go international they hook up with the ISID, International Security Identification Division. This global networking system includes Paine Webber which has thousands of corporations. Some of the people in these corporations are the major stock holders of the privatized company CCA, Correction Corporations of America, and they are heavily involved with Fanny Mae and Freddy Mack. The REI, Real Estate Investment Trust, and PZN, Prison Realty Trust, are companies that have also become privatized. They eat tremendously off of the prison system.

This credit and debt system is ran by UNICITRAL, United Nations Convention on International Trade Law. This corporation is owned by the United Nations and it also includes the Jesuits, the Vatican, the Roman

Catholic Church, and the Pentagon. The criminal justice system is all commercial and it's designed to continue slavery and make profit off of human beings. It was set up from the beginning to destroy the African American nation.

Can you imagine if just half of the troubled people in America decided to do other careers besides criminal careers? The jail and prison population would start to decline and the government would be highly upset because the prison system is one of largest money makers in the world. They probably would come up with another solution for lack of crime. A traumatic solution like Operation Depopulation.

Citizen Vs Felon

If you have a clean criminal record you are considered a good person and a model citizen. You only receive a record when you are accused of a crime, convicted of a crime or start making a career in criminal activity. If the police accuses you of a crime you are in the beginning stages but if you advance your criminal career and receive a felony conviction, you receive an F on your report card of life. Once a convicted felon no matter the charge, the white legal system attempts to separate you from other citizens because you are a felon and considered a bad seed. You will always be judged unjustly by your fellow citizens. Some of these citizens are the employers that control whether you are able to take care of your family or not. You will always be looked at as a bad person even if you're truly a good person who made a bad decision. This is how it begins:

If you become unlucky and get arrested by the police, you begin to start a social following in the criminal justice system. If you continue to get in trouble and finally get a felony record, your entire life changes because your record has transformed you in the eyes of America. This record follows you and determines what the general public thinks of you. You really are no longer a citizen even if you pay taxes and work for minimum wage. Becoming a felon or ex-convict is really like receiving a degree. You have earned a degree in Nothingness.

Having a drug or sex case enhances the degree to master or doctorate level. You are unemployable, unable to rent an apartment, no school funding, no government funding, you become the unseen citizen eligible for nothing. Although when you are released from prison, house arrest or probation, the law states you have paid your debt to society. This is far from true.

Once you are released, you fall into more debt or old habits because of your degree in Nothingness. You might do something criminal because you have to eat and this act lands you in prison or back in prison. This place is called the Department of Correction but really it's the Department of Corruption. They have taken most of the education programs out of prison so you're forced to learn from other convicts, who may teach you how to be a better convict.

After years of hearing stories, watching people fight, watching people die and years of watching homosexual male officers and offenders, you finally get out and don't know what to do with your life. This is where the 75% residual return rate comes in and please don't get the habitual!

Until you figure out that your actions must change, you will continue to have the same results. You have to work harder, do something greater and be something better than an American citizen because after you become a felon, a citizen is something you really no longer are. Nothingness belongs to you until you recognize your strengths and God given talents and make those work for you. Being a criminal is not a talent it's a curse.

The white man has brainwashed some into believing the only way that they can obtain the fake American dream, is through criminal and corrupt acts. Sell drugs and you can come up in the neighborhood, sport fancy clothes, put 28's on your truck, have lots of women and take care of your family. They don't tell you of the corruption of the other black family that buys from you and loses everything from buying the drugs you sell. Robbing, killing and stealing from your neighbor destroys your family and keeps black on black crime relevant and prevalent in our communities.

We must walk away from the acts that continue to house the criminal justice system with black fathers and mothers. We must find a way to change Nothingness into everything.

The Police

When you think of gangs which gangs do you immediately think about? Let's see Crips, Bloods, Disciples, Vice Lords, Blackstone's, Sir 13, Latin kings, Black mafia, Italian mafia, Mexican mafia, Hells Angels, Outlaws, Pagans, Sons of Silence, Aryan Nation, Baptist, Pentecostal, Methodist, Apostolic, Coptic, Shiite, Sunni, The Nation, Jehovah Witness, Moors, Hebrew, Kemites, Judaist, Buddhist, the list is extremely long and depends on what you have been programmed to believe what is required to be considered a gang. Contrary to popular belief, a gang is an extended family that comes together and partakes in different activities. Gangs claim control over a specific territory.

Street gangs rob people, sell drugs, extort from businesses, murder people and fight with rival gang members for turf, colors, stripes, money, women and so on. These street gangs are tough but they are nothing compared to the largest organized gang in the world and unfortunately they do the exact same criminal acts but have the power to get away with it.

I would be referring to the police and all of the other unions and institutions. Street gangs such as the Black Panthers and the Guardian Angels stood for the greater good. They fought against those who withheld certain rights from black people. These rights were violated by the higher up political powers, the police department and white supremacist.

Black American destruction resulted from the combination of poverty, poor public housing, lack of education, feelings of hopelessness, family abuse and the 1970's, 80's and 90's drug trafficking operation under the white power umbrella. Neighborhoods became polluted with crime from blacks trying to obtain the fake white American dream. The police and fake politicians came in posing as the good ole boys to save the day but made matters worse. Do you not know that they are a gang?

The first police force in America was created by the great inventor and businessman Ben Franklin. Through-out the years, police have been white racist, violators of the constitution and some were and still are Klan's men. They have an unlimited amount of weapons, transportation, communication technology and paper to write any kind of false affidavit they wish. The police will look at you with a straight face and insurmountable lies and leave you with no defense. They are the physical prosecutors and judges of the law and they will manipu-late, misuse and abuse the law.

I personally have been the victim of police many times. I've been lied on by the police about my driver's license that was valid. I've been hit in the head with a military style weapon, which resulted in my blood being splattered all over my girlfriend's bathroom. This left a forever mark on the right side of my head. The report said I sustained a cut on the toilet, not true. I was brutalized and jabbed in the back with the same military rifle. They wanted to kill me but thank God for the supervisor that came in and stopped this certain officer that was about to kick all my teeth out.

I've been tasered with handcuffs on longer than 6 seconds. I've been punched in my mouth multiple times and lost a tooth. I've been slammed on my face on the concrete and called a nigger multiple times by the police. The police are supposed to be our public servants upholding the law under God and the constitution but sometimes certain ones break every law. This makes them worse than harden criminals. The laws that American citizens obey are arranged for the police to be above them.

Take for instance the RICO act, which means Racketeering Influenced Corrupt Organization. This charge and the charges conspiracy and dealing, makes it legal for police or the FBI to investigate an individual or individuals and attempt to do controlled buys. They build their cases by receiving information from haters, neighbors, family members and so called friends. The police can legally give these citizens, corporate informants or snitches small or large amounts of money, drugs or weapons to sell or purchase and it's totally legal. Of course it is not legal so prison here you come.

After they present their information to a magistrate judge they receive their most exiting document, the no knock warrant. They now turn into full fledge military soldiers to take down citizens turned terrorists and they love it! After they illegally set you up, they can kick in your door, beat you, shoot you, use attack dogs, ignite flash bombs use chemical agents, confiscate property, vehicles, electronics, jewelry, drugs, bank accounts and some of this merchandise is used for their personal use.

Some of the police are American terrorists. I say this because of their use of excessive force which in many cases results in innocent citizens and animals being shot, beat, killed, choked or suffering heart attacks. These legal American terrorist then change into prosecuting lawyers in the courtroom and help convict millions of innocent people by writing up false affidavits. After all of this they turn around and do it all over again, just another day in the life of a public servant. Now who sounds like a corrupt organization and gang?

The NYPD gives an example of these corrupt ones. NYPD officers Eppolito and Caracappa committed many racketeering acts and murders for Italian mafia. They were caught and convicted but many are still out here operating. The police have a blood oath to stick together just like street gangs, whether it's justice or injustice.

In 2014 some NYPD officers turned their backs on their mayor. He was giving a speech supporting the death of two officers that were murdered. The mayor who is white, has an African American wife and son. He criticized officers who use excessive force. These two murders were acts of retaliation from the chocking death of an unarmed black man. You must remember, most of the law makers were white racists so there will always be some hatred towards black people.

The white law called stand your ground has influenced many law enforcement officers and citizens to kill black people. This law was brought to light after the murder of Travon Martin, a young unarmed black man. White policemen are killing up black people across America like it's the law. To them it is the law, to kill all black-men. The police and other racist civilians have been brainwashed into believing that they can kill black people when they get scared.

They choke us; we say "We can't breathe" they say "I know you can breathe and you're a nigger, we hate niggers." Then we die. We hold our hands up unarmed stating "Don't shoot" they shoot first and say "You being black automatically makes you armed and dangerous, I'm white and my years of police training leads me to defend my life with force, especially from niggers, we want all niggers to die."

What would happen if black people start standing their ground and killing white people when they get scared? I guarantee the results would not be the same.

The police gang will continue to be a threat and if we were to put up a good fight against the powers that be, they'll just bring in the National Guard, the Army, Navy, Air force, Marines, FBI, FEMA, CIA, Homeland Security or any other government gang unit used to keep the oppressed under control. The police are really modern day slave masters who have upgraded their weapons from whips, ropes and chains into guns, mace, taser and bombs. They are the physical judges that have the power to change your entire life for the worst. They are the beginning of you entering the Criminal system and becoming a felon. So be careful.

CIA

The Central Intelligence Agency is the most mysterious agency in the world. The George Bush Center in Virginia is where the headquarters is located and they have always been involved in all kinds of weird experiments and research. They connect to DARPA, Defense Advanced Research Projects Agency and together they have created some of the most mindboggling projects in the world. MKULTRA, Project Monarch, and other high-tech programs like HARP and ECHELON are also connected to the CIA.

MKULTRA is the project that is strictly mind control. It started by using extreme interrogation tactics that advanced after the USA moved Nazi scientist from Germany. This movement was called Operation Paper Clip. Nazi scientists were extremely intelligent and one of them invented a machine in a basement that simulated nuclear fusion. American scientist grew in knowledge from these Nazi scientists.

Under MKULTRA, scientists used military soldiers, prisoners, mental patients and volunteers like research monkeys. Of the many things used were hypnosis, drugs, electroshock, radiation, radio waves, hypnotism and other psychiatric and bio chemical techniques. They even have implanted electronic devices in the brain that trigger controlled commands when activated by a code word, cell phone or remote control. So someone could be a normal person living a normal life and all a sudden that person could snap and go into a school, concert or movie theater then +++.

This information kind of makes you second guess previous bombings, explosions, assassinations and terrorist attacks. President John F. Kennedy said a speech about the involvement of the CIA and other societies. He was later assassinated. His demise was very mysterious and his whole role as president was very similar to Abraham Lincoln. They both supported black people, they both knew confidential information and they both were trying to ease the money system. These three things are probably what got them knocked off.

The CIA's Project Pegasus is a project that's like way out there. Project Pegasus started when the CIA began to receive foreign information which increased their knowledge. They began advancing in technology in extremely high levels. This project deals with time travel, teleportation and visitations to other planets.

The Stairgate Program is a program that allows CIA agents to look through crystals and communicate with other beings and have out of body experiences to retrieve information from other locations. It is rumored that with this powerful technology, all natural events in the past, present and future have the possibility to be observed or visited. . If this is true, then they probably knew about the Trade Center event in the 60's or 70's.

It is also rumored that there are "jumper" locations where agents can jump to another place in time or space, a place like Mars. Attorney Andrew Basiago said he's been a part of the program Project Pegasus since he was a small child. He is the son of a high ranking CIA agent and he said that he went back in time and witnessed Abraham Lincoln's Gettysburg Address. He also said that he has "jumped" to Mars. There he saw and spoke to humanoid like creatures. One of these "jumper" locations is rumored to be the big apple New York.

The CIA is a foreign company with super information so don't rule all the things mentioned in this chapter topic out. I only scraped the surface. They are at least 500 years ahead of the general public with intelligence, information and technology thanks to World War 2 and the world's best physicist, chemist, hypnotist, scientists, engineers and computer geniuses. The CIA is a scientific gang.

True Freemasons

Of all the organized gangs in the world, I believe the Freemasons are the heart that connects them altogether. It's the one that's out in the open for the public to see, so it's not a secret. They have lodges that are spread out across the world. Thousands of people claim that they are masons. Doctors, lawyers, judges, public servants, preachers even the average Joe the plumber. You may know a mason, you may even be a mason but you may not know about the many secrets rituals and their main purpose. It runs deeper than sporting the G symbol on your clothing jewelry or automobile. It's also more to it than having mason meetings and parties or having a couple of special coins to get you out of trouble. Their history is quite educating. I will now explain what I have uncovered about those who are called the Freemasons and this information is only about the true elite ark Freemasons. They are beyond accepted and free because they're white.

The true American Freemasons are directly connected to Germany and the Bavarian Illuminati. Their first lodge came into existence in the 1700's in England. After the alliance of Adam Weishupt of the

Illuminati and Baron Von Kinnge of the Freemasons, the masonic order took form in America.

The founding fathers of America were Freemasons including George Washington, who was a master mason of Virginia and Ben Franklin, who was a master mason of Pennsylvania. John Hancock was also a mason and he was president of the Continental Congress and had the largest signature on the Declaration of Independence. These men owned hundreds of slaves while declaring freedom to all men violating the entire constitution.

The Freemason's doctrines are called rites of order and the most important rites are the Scottish rite and the York rite. The Scottish rite can go all the way up to the 33rd degree and if you get that far, you would find out some deep secrets. The York rite has 3 additional levels and one main level is the Knights Templar. The Knights Templar comes from the stories of the Knights that accompanied the pilgrims from Europe to Egypt, during the Crusades. They gained immense wealth from the treasures they stolen and later they had to leave their homes and flee to Scotland when King Philip ordered them to be tortured on Friday the 13.th

The American and French revolutions along with the Great Orient of France, brought the Scottish rite to America. This victorious event led the French to give America the gift the statue of liberty, who in 1865 represented the fake freedom of slaves after the civil war. This statue was first a black woman and was transformed into a white woman who actually is a pagan god and a symbol of Babylon.

New York became New York because of the York Rite and the city York that is in England. Since America was the New World, New York became the headquarters of many empires. From the New York stock exchange, to the New York Trade center, to the New York Rockefellers, to the real estate king of New York, Republican presidential candidate front runner Donald Trump, New York New York.

The Blue lodge is the most common lodge in America and Canada and there are 3 levels in becoming a mason in the blue lodge. The initiation is quite crazy if you ask me. The first level is an apprentice, the second level is fellow craft and the third level is master. The initiation goes like this: First you have to change clothes and have all your money taken out of your pockets. You have to be blindfolded and be held captive in darkness until you find your way to the light and then you are set free. You are now illuminated to a new being.

The Freemason probates have tools that they earn during completing each level. The tools consist of the apron which is really a dress. The compass, the carpenters square, the gauge and the gavel. The letter G is the signature letter and stands for geometry or The Great or Grand Architect of the Universe. You must believe in some form of religion or higher power and the Bible is sometimes used. Ok now here comes the weird stuff. The higher power and the G can stand for Lucifer, Satan or the devil if satanic worship is your chosen religion.

The Freemasons organization is based on the theory and legend of the architect Hiram Abiff. This master craftsmen was sent to King Solemn by a man who also was named Hiram. He is the king of Tryee. The two kings made a peace treaty and they traded gold, wheat, wood, oils and labor. This is the trinity of the Freemasons. King Solomon, King Hiram of Tryee and Hiram Abiff. The legend goes on to say that after Hiram Abiff was sent to King Solomon, he reportedly had sex

with one of Solomon's wives. King Solomon then sent
the 3 Jews to ruff him up a little but they ended up
killing him. Hiram Abiff supposedly raises from the dead
and enters into the afterlife like Jesus Christ.
What's funny about this trinity is that the King of
Tyree is spiritually compared to Lucifer in the Bible,
because of his pride, riches, trafficking and wanting to
be God. This is in Ezekiel 28.The money transactions to
King Solemn also resemble a connection to Lucifer
because the yearly amount of gold he received was 666
talents. This is in 1st Kings 10:14. My question is why
would any good virtue organization pay homage to one
of their core representatives, who in the Bible is
described as Lucifer?

The Freemason's probates who reach an advanced
level have to recite the three death confessions that
were told to King Solomon by the 3 Jews.
The first one said "cut out my tongue
The second one said "cut out my heart
The third one said "cut my body in half
This is totally sick. Freemasons have secret
handshakes just like street gangs and they also run
under letters, stars, colors and codes just like street
gangs. What most people don't understand is that the
Freemasons and other societies were practicing these
things hundreds of years before street gangs. So street
gangs really copy the actions, methods and symbols of
organizations like the Freemasons. I mean where do you
think the concept and every aspect of an organized
gang comes from?

They worship under the 6 and 5point stars just like
the street organizations the Disciples and Vice Lords.
People think that the 6 point star the hexagram, is the
Star of David and people have considered it holy. It is

the current star of Israel but the 6 point star has nothing to do with King David. Its reference to him worshiping this star or being his star, is found nowhere in the Bible.

This dual triangular star is used to communicate in higher levels and is connected to the worship of Lucifer. Its dimensions are the number of the beast and man, the numbers are 666. Star worship was a Babylonian religion that was practiced during the time of King Solomon.

God condemns worship to any graven image and he charged men because of their personal worship to stars and other gods. Read Amos 5:26 and Acts 7:43. Later in time, Adolph Hitler who corrupted the swastika gave the Jews the 6 point star as an official sign to remind them of pain and death. The Holocaust which means burnt offering, was the event when Hitler forced the Jews to wear a yellow 6 point star upon their clothing, then burning them to death in the furnace. Hitler's gift of the 6 point star, is like giving African Americans a flag that has a noose on it. This is total humiliation and dehumanization.

The 5 point star the pentagram, is also a star that's used to summon demons and do satanic rituals. This star and its mathematical dimensions make up the American military's headquarters the Pentagon. It's the symbol of law enforcement and many government and non-government corporations. This star also is part of the Baphomet the Satanic he/she goat. If you research the images of the Baphomet, you will find that he/she makes the same hand signs that George Washington and Jesus Christ makes. This reveals their masonic plan of church, LGBT and state.

Freemasons have even more symbols like the pyramid, the all seeing-eye, the owl, the eagle and the scales and balance. Some of these symbols can be seen printed on American green currency. Sandusky Ohio and of course Washington DC are the two cities that have the most masonic imagery. Many rap, r-n-b, rock and pop artist have these symbols all through their videos and they are in plenty of TV shows and movies as well. The Freemason influence the entire entertainment industry. They can build any business they desire.

If you are a True Freemason, Arch Freemason, Prince Hall Freemason, Eastern Star or a Shriner and you're true and God fearing then peace be upon you. But if you're in to worshipping the devil and having sex with children and animals, drinking their blood and sacrificing humans then you have a serious problem and may God not have mercy on your soul.

The book of Revelation 18 speaks of the rich and powerful people that drink from the cup of the satanic whore, Queen Lucifer who represents modern day Babylon, Americas New York City. The Angel yelled out twice, Babylon has fallen complimenting the two towers that fell. It's just a matter of time that the enemy will be revealed.

Illuminati, 911 and the Media

To have a chapter about the Freemasons and not have a chapter about the Illuminati, would be like having a body without blood. When you look at a person you just see the body. You don't see the blood unless the body gets cut open. Well I'm about to do some cutting.

The Illuminati is the blood that is in the Freemasons. It's the society that's slightly hush hush even though millions may talk about it these days, due to Google and

YouTube. The research that I have done on the Illuminati is my interpretation of the information that I have gathered through these same searching tools and various books that I've read. There are many corporations that are the Illuminati and many that are involved with the Illuminati. Most of these individuals in these major corporations are American, British, German, Jewish but some are Asian and even African.

There many branches of the Illuminati and Freemason governments. The Illuminati is the secret power that's behind politics and most governments, local and foreign. Its power connects people who you think are your friends, to people who you think are your enemies or former enemies. This is why the UN is a branch of 6 super powers that consist of the United States, Britain, France, Russia, Germany and China. I personally added Germany because their Nazi power is involved with the Illuminati in more ways than you could possibly think. The Illuminati run the world and the world's money system. It's rumored that two families of these Illuminati branches have enough wealth to feed the entire world. These two families are the Roths and the Rocks.

The birth of the Illuminati in America was May 1st 1776. This was the same year that freedom was declared from the British. The Illuminati money system started in the early 17 and 1800's, not to long after the integration of the Illuminati and the Freemason governments.

The Jacobians founder Jacob Schiff, left Germany and came to New York with the blueprints to control the money system. Being backed with the money of the house of Rothschild, he was able to overthrow governments. He previously overthrew governments of Russia and the French.

When he arrived in America he made a partnership with Albert Pike. This helped Mr. Jacob connect the Bank of America, JP Morgan, Paul Walberg, the Rockefellers and other affiliates into a gigantic money making conspiracy. The people in these corporations own the banks, run the town and all of the money is theirs. The money system took shape in America in the early 1900's from the force of politics and white true Freemasons. Under the watchful eye of Edward Mandel a high British official, Woodrow Wilson was automatically made president. All presidents are selected, not elected.

Eventually came the Federal Reserve Act which connects to the most criminal amendment in the Constitution, the16th amendment. The Federal Act paved the way for the coming of the Illuminati and Freemason green paper money system. The Federal Act was overseen by the Federal Reserve Party. This party consisted of 13 reserve members, 12 bank members and 1 member of the Federal Board.

The Illuminati and Freemasons favorite 6 numbers are 1, 5, 6, 11, 13, 33, and 13 is their Powerball number because the power of 13 controls all the green currency in the entire country, as you will see in the next chapter.

The one dollar bill is the main bank note that promotes worldwide white imperialism. The message to the world of the power of the 13 is printed on the dollar bill. On it is 13 stars, 13 stripes, 13 steps to the top of the Egyptian pyramid that was built on 13 acres, 13 berries, 13 arrows, 13 leaves, and 13 letters over the pyramid that mean, *he has favored our undertakings,* 13 letters on the ribbon that's in the eagle's mouth that mean, *out of many, one.* There were 13 colonies in the union, there is a council of 13, they own the 13 most powerful states, there are 13 main banks,13 is the number of witches that meet to cast satanic spells, there is a 13th zodiac sign that's reptilian, Oh! Let's not forget the 13th amendment that connects directly to black slavery and white slave masters.

On the one dollar bill is also President George Washington who was a true master mason and a slave master. On the back of the dollar above the pyramid, is the All Seeing Eye which was the Eye of Horus but on the dollar it's transformed into an all seeing European eye or reptilian eye. The little owl and the alien on the dollar are also strange but the real message on the dollar are the letters under the pyramid, *Novus Ordo Seclorum,* A new Order of the Ages. This is The New World Order.

This message reveals the worldwide undertaking that was favored by him, their GAOTU Lucifer. The one dollar bill reveals the Illuminati's plan with symbols that come from the secret knowledge that they stole from Africa. On the 100 dollar bill is the man who was not a president but was a great inventor, businessman and also a true master mason and slave master. Everybody in America wants a lot of him in their pockets and bank accounts. The Great Depression opened the door for President Roosevelt to bring in The New Deal.

The New Deal allows the government to print money, take a percentage of the money, watch the money, insure the money and when the government spends too much money, takes too much money and borrows too much money, they can simply propose a bill and print some more money. It's all about the money because money controls people. The makers of the money belong to government branches who are controlled by the Illuminati true Freemasons.

They are the overseers of mostly all the corporations and businesses in the world, on and off the record. The Supreme Court of the United States of America has specialized terminology for these many corporations they call them persons! They also have a unique name for the money that they have; they call the money speech because big money talks loud and in different languages.

Under the web of the Illuminati and Freemasons is the corporation called the Council on Foreign Relations? It was once called the League of Nations, and the headquarters was in Switzerland, which is the same place that the World Wide Web started, and it's where CERN is located. Once the name was changed the headquarters was changed to modern day Babylon New York. The building for the council was built with funding from John Rockefeller.

New York City comes up a lot in this book and the trade center tragedy also does. This is because New York is one of the Illuminati's main headquarters and the trade center event is the largest planned money making strategy in the history of America. I will go into great detail about the fakeness and mind manipulation of 911.

All the media is controlled by their white power, so certain things are filtered. Understand that there is an organized strategy about all news. The idea is to control the universal energy of how people feel. You're either sad, angry, happy or scared when you watch the news. The news leads millions of people into believing anything that is broadcasted. The media giants know that the general public are gullible, and they look at the news as gospel.

So if a news reporter, president, celebrity, preacher or any other influential person says dogs can speak English like humans, and they produce a couple of fake visual images, a large percentage of the general public will believe that dogs can talk English like humans. Soon as the word is out on the news, people start posting on Facebook, texting, tweeting and calling everybody and now the rumor is history. Sometimes the media will leak out secret information, but you got to be on it because they only show secrets once and as quick as possible.

So back to 911. I'm going to show you that this event was planned and orchestrated. If you believe that terrorists attacked America Sept.11 2001, please pay attention: The day was Sept.10 and Rumsfeld announces that the government was trillions in debt and war was declared against the Pentagon. They were accused of stealing the money. President George Bush later proposed a defense bill for billions of dollars; I guess to try and replace some of the money that the government stole from itself. This is mass confusion. The war against America was a money situation, and the terrorist was the American military.

The next day on Sept.11 the entire nationwide news covered the so called terrorist attack. Two planes hit the top of the trade center twin towers. People were set on fire, people jumped out of buildings, a lot of people died. Hundreds of people, police and firefighters said they heard bombs blowing the building up from the bottom. Hot iron was seen on the bottom. Tons of gold supposedly came up missing from the bottom. Local authorities later were restricted from the bottom, all at ground 0.

A magical explosion happened at the Pentagon with no concrete evidence of any aircraft. Then a large mysterious airplane was seen flying over the White House during all this terror. No one supposedly knows anything about the plane or who's on it. All this happens to the country with the most advanced and powerful military in the world?

No, not in this world! The American military is an atomic force on this earth! They have weapon and surveillance technology that you wouldn't believe. Most of the American public was so focused on the tragedy that they didn't pay attention to what the media said the super military did on 911. You must not forget that the media told you that they stole over 2 trillion dollars the day before 911. They were doing test runs with aircraft the same day of 911. They allowed two planes to fly into two buildings and let another plane fly over the White House without shooting it down. The American military would never allow that, and you know it. Not in this world. You're not getting it, pay more attention. Enter the media and the Bushes.

Marvin Bush, George Bush's little brother, was the principal of the security company. He was over the trade center, United airlines and the Dulles airport. On this day, 2 Bushes controlled the entire security of corporate America. Under their watch thousands died, and thousands were injured. President Bush announces on national news that the attacks were made by an Islamic terrorist group, and it's time to go to war. The military is going to find the Muslim leader Osama Bin Laden and kill him. This is where those 100 billion dollar bills come in. America is in the red zone and now under attack by terrorists.

Two years later on the day of one of the favorite Illuminati Freemasons numbers, the 13th of December, President Bush announces on the news "we got him." But him is not who we were looking for. Bush and the media influenced the general public to stop the primary focus of fear and terror of Osama Bin Laden and switch the focus to Saddam Hussein. He eventually was sentenced to death by hanging with the help of the good ole U.S.A. The media never broadcasted Saddam as a suspect of 911 until Bush's announcement three years later. This lets us know that this is a family revenge situation because George Bush Sr. previously did the Contra weapons for drugs operation with Saddam Hussein.

Nancy told us to say no to drugs while her husband and Daddy Bush was selling them. Shall I remind you that George Bush Sr. is who announced the New World Order on Sept. 11, 1991, letting you know that 911 is part of the New Order, and it's the success that he predicted they would have.

George Bush Jr. accused Hussein of aiding the suspect terrorist group with weapons of mass destruction. Weapons that he got from his father back in the day. The first terrorist group the American military is never mentioned for some reason. They're the ones that war was declared upon in the first place. This is mass confusion; there's even more!

Fast forward eight years on the day after Illuminati birthday, President Obama announces on national news that the military found and killed Osama Bin Laden. The same man that the American military and George Bush

Jr. had been looking for all these years. America is now supposed to cut the focus of fear and anger back on Osama but can't cause it's been so may years, and we forgot. This information came out of nowhere just like the planes that hit the tower and the magical explosion of the Pentagon. There's even more. At the end of 2014, the media reported that tactics that the military used on captured 911 terrorists, were not effective and didn't produce any new information? What new information? I thought the 911 case was closed. Would you like to know what 911 was really about?

911 was all about making money and declaring wars! War creates the government. Tragedy creates more money for the government. Listen to what this tragedy did: The World Trade Center catastrophe briefly destroyed foreign trading, which created new systems. New bills were proposed and new currency was printed, new buildings were built, new wars were declared, and brand new security scanning systems were placed in all county buildings across the country. Taxes were increased which affected the prices of primary commodities like gold, gas, oil, food, raised prices on illegal products like marijuana, cocaine, and heroin. 911 was a physiological weapon which forced people to believe and depend on the government for help and protection from a terrorist group that never came in the country with guns and bombs a blazing.

This brainwashed threat was present in the American mind due to the media. What dominant country travels to other countries with guns and bombs bursting in the air, trying to govern, help govern or confiscate weapons? Who dropped a nuclear atomic bomb that killed thousands of men, women and children?

Osama Bin Laden, Saddam Hussein, Mummar Gaddafi, even today's ISIS have never done terrorist acts like America has done to other countries, but the media has a multitude of people believing that they have. The power that controls the media is the illuminati. The power that controls the money is the Illuminati. The power that controls the world is the Illuminati. They are a rich white man racist gang.

13 Most Powerful States

Boston Massachusetts, New York New York, Philadelphia Pennsylvania, Cleveland Ohio, Richmond Virginia, Atlanta Georgia, Chicago Illinois, St. Louis and Kansas City Missouri, Minneapolis Minnesota, Dallas Texas, and San Francisco California. These are the 12 states, and if you letter them, they are A-L. These states and cities command and influence the entire world in more ways than you possibly imagine. They connect to everything that has ever happened in America.

Racism, slavery, freedom, drugs, money, music, the stock market, 911, technology, LGBT, almost anything you can possibly think about is connected in one way or another to one of these 12 cities or states. These states own America, and they're responsible for the formation of America.

Pay attention to your local media and you will find that these states report the most major murders, the most LGBT promotion, the most celebrity and music promotion and the most modern financial broadcasting. There are many reasons for all the violent acts that have infected America. It has become polluted demonically and chemically. These infections affect the minds of many Americans which is why it easy for some to turn into rabid wild dogs. There have been more killings in my hometown than ever. These things are happening because of so much pollution.

We all are being polluted from the air, from food, from music, TV, ourselves and others, chemical trails, free immunization shots, medications and the bomb making material that's in our bleach smelling drinking water and toothpaste. The decisions for all these things are enforced by the powers that occupy one of these 12 states. These states are part of the pollution because they influence the entire population of America to thirst for their power. They have the power because they own all of the money and print all the money. This money sometimes corrupts us more than anything on this earth because we sometimes fall in love with the money.

1st Timothy 6:10 tells us that the love of money is the root of all evil and all of the evil in the earth comes from its master the devil. This particular scripture goes on to say that loving money will make you leave your faith and cause yourself many sorrows. Their power is in the money, and it's all about the money. They know that from birth to death, somebody is going to be spending some of their money.

Everybody wants and needs money and when you get the money it doesn't even belong to you. You don't own your money, because if you did, couldn't no federal state or IRS agent take it with just cause. It would belong to you and only you, and it would have your serial numbers on it so you can track it. We really just use money like the monopoly game. The only difference is the bank don't start you out with a dime. The paper money system is the white masonic system, and it's all about secrets, orders, and numbers. This is why the12 cities and states connect directly to the law of the

Federal Reserve Act. The Federal Reserve Act was overseen by the Federal Reserve Party.

These 12 cities and states represent the Federal Reserve Act that had 13 members, but there are only 12 states. The truth is there are 13 states, and the 13th state is Washington DC. It's neither a city nor a state. It's in a federal district of its own, so it stands alone. These are what these 13 cities and states are in full detail. The 12 cities of these states are the 12 bank members of the United States Federal Reserve. These 12 banks oversee all the money. The 13th state is the one member of the Federal Reserve board, and it oversees the 12 states. The 13th state is the most powerful because it sovereign just like the Vatican and its home to the largest white plantation in the United States. Its oval office mirrors the St. Peter's Square in the Vatican and they both face an obelisk which they have adopted from ancient Egypt.

The American citizens don't understand that the federal District of Columbia is the elite white slave master. This means the citizens are just modern indentured servants and wards of the state. These 13 cities and states are the true Freemasons and the Illuminati's roots to all evil, and big money is the root. The 12 states house a federal reserve bank that prints the money and controls the money movement in the entire United States, which is in the trillions. The 13th state watches all the money in all 50 states. That is too much money!

Good money, bad money, church money, drug money, blood money and dirty money, it's all mixed in together. The love of money is the root to all evil and when evil is present, the devil Lucifer is also. This is why the last city's letter is an L for Lucifer, but the 13th city's letter is M for money! The first city is where it all began, no taxation without representation.

The last two cities are where it all ends with Silicon Valley and the White House. The money is the power of the illuminati, and the negative energy of all the dirty money is causes turbulence throughout the country. They can put a black face on their money but understand that it's only more the reason to raise children in identifying black people as freed 20 dollar slaves and white people as 20 million dollar slave masters. This is the Black Truth-911- The Illuminati.

All American Terrorist

There are numerous nationwide hate crimes killing Africans Americans across the country. These crimes are committed by the white man police officers. Not only do certain men of the law practice theses hate crimes towards black people, some of the white American citizens agree with the cops with the negative influence to hate black people and kill them. The satanic alliance of different brotherhoods continue with the plan of total annihilation and genocide to all African Americans. This is proof that the white man is a brilliant all-American terrorist. The demonic spirit of racial discrimination and the dehumanization of black people has possessed some of those who say they're our friends. They are not our friends; they are our enemies. Plain and simply put.

These people are in white supremacy gangs, and they are the real terrorist who terrorizes the nation and causes the government to make changes to the laws that waste billions of tax dollars. These white powered terrorist come in all ages, positions, and places and they are not playing about their loyalty to the white devil to kill. They do these things in the name of Lucifer and white Jesus.

The Confederates, KKK, and other white supremacy groups are terrorist, murderers and killers. These people are America's Isis, but you may not think so because you listen to the media and think these kinds of people have mental problems or they may have had a bad day and just flipped out and killed everybody. No! These people are pure evil! These people have the devil himself in them! They are microchipped, medicated or programmed to hate.

These people are the white man! And the white man is not flesh and blood! The white man is a worldly power and negative energy. Their entire racist principality is trained to have hatred towards black people, and they have a love to commit senseless murders and multiple hate crimes. These white racist terrorist are devils.

The definition of the devil is a doer of evil and evil is the energy that flows through the veins of these white racists. In the 1920's, they performed black genocide in the town of Tulsa Oklahoma. The terrorist group the KKK and other white racists stopped the beginning of the first Black American economic enterprise. They bombed the place and set the entire town on fire, including all the black businesses and left thousands dead, homeless and in the penitentiary. Then in the 1960's, they committed more murders including four little black girls, Evans, Martin, Malcolm, even two Kennedys back to back. These racist acts are similar to the ones that were committed in Charleston SC.

This racist state is the state that a white police officer gunned down an unarmed black man and killed him like a very weak man because he shot him in his back. In this same town, a young white man entered a predominantly black African American church during Bible study. He listened to the word of God for an hour and decided to kill the church pastor and eight other members, including women.

The pastor of the church Clementa Pinckey, served the city of Charleston SC as an African American politician. When the police officer detained the young white terrorist, he received a bulletproof vest and a bond hearing from his white man brothers. I call them brothers because the white officer would have killed a black terrorist on site if he committed the same terrorist acts. The young white supremacist gets a break and doesn't even get beat up, tased, maced, or shot. He obtains a bond and smiles for the camera.

When something this serious awaken you, you realize that the real terrorists are not Islamic militants from the Middle East. The real terrorists are your white American citizens who hate black people so much that they wanna flip out and kill them. Some of these terrorists are your neighbors that live right next door to you and their sweetest joy is to shoot men in the back, blow up places where there will be a large gathering, burn down black churches or go in them and kill black people. These people have the same spirit as the slave masters and conquerors back in the 17 and 1800's.

People must understand that there is never really been an Islamic terrorist threat to put the country in the red zone. Until some foreign military force drops soldiers and bombs in America, there ain't no damn terrorists. The white media has been putting white lies in your mind. It's time to wake up and do something about this problem now.

The terrorists that you should fear are not over there in the Middle East. The real terrorists are right here in the good ole U. S. of A and guess what, they're all American.

PART X Movement to One Nation
The Message

This message goes out to my young men, the ones we call thugs. The ones in the neighborhood who think they are so tough. I feel this chapter topic needs to be heard especially after talking to a couple of young men I know personally. Please excuse the language in this section. I only use choice words to describe the character of some of the hard head youngsters of the world. A lot of youngsters feel that can't nobody tell them anything. They don't understand that they are in a state of unconsciousness, and it's time to wake up! Spike Lee depicted our state of unconsciousness best in his movie School Daze. Do you understand young men that you're doing exactly what the white supremacist want you to do? Do you know what that is?

They want you to continue to be dumb, ignorant, uneducated, selfish, prideful, lustful, aggressive, lovers of money, crime and drugs. Something is terribly wrong with my young men who act like thugs all the time. A young man told me that he thought about robbing his aunt because she had a little money. Another one said he dropped out of school because school and good grades are for lames. Another one said he contemplated killing his brother for not sharing his wealth from drug sells and then there was the one that said he was going to get mamma tried tattooed on his eyelids. What in the hell has become of my young black brothers in America?

This attitude is why America has more people in prison than any other place in the world. Black folk out number all races that are in prison, even though in all crimes more whites are initially arrested. I believe this happens because of the many white laws that were made to enslave black people. The powers that be know that their mind control operation is working fine.

This operation is in the power of the music. As I said before the music of the past spoke love, the music of today speaks nothing of love. In the past when people used to take pictures they used to throw up the peace sign and now they're throwing up the middle finger. Young people are not raised to respect themselves anymore. They don't respect their peers, parents, teachers, women, God, old folk or their children. Most young folks are rude, high on drugs and disturbed. When there is a small problem, instead of fighting they rather grab the AK. In some cases when protection of family and kids are involved, a gun is a great answer but most of the times a simple ass whipping is all that is needed.

Men refuse to accept an ass whipping especially when it is one who thinks he's tough, thinks he's a boss or he has a little money. This is why for seven months straight, me and my shorty's used to eat food and watch Cubes Visions Friday every Friday. The message was when you have a problem with a man you use your fists, and you live to fight another day. Another message about this same subject was given by old-school rapper Kool Moe Dee. In his song The Wild, Wild West, the lyrics state "Guns we don't like to use them unless our enemies choose em' we prefer to fight you all like a man and beat you down with our hands and body slam you."

I know this is prehistoric compared to this day and age but damn, if some of the street codes of the past still could be here today, there probably would be a lot more young people still alive. Black on black murders will never change until the messages change. As I said before, the message is in the music and the movies. The message from most of the songs today is money; guns, drinks, drugs, sex, power, forget about knowledge. If you ask the average three young men what their favorite movie is, one out three will say Scarface, the cocaine king. If you ask the same three neighborhood men who is their favorite rapper, not one of them will say Common, who in 2015 along with John Legend, won an Oscar award for best song Glory.

Young thugs love trap music, and it has become exactly what it is. A trap to keep you inside. When you are trapping, you're either winning or losing. Winning in the trap means living good, eating good, drinking good, smoking good, sexing good, riding good, dressing good and big money in your pocket and possession. This is the trap that the rappers rap about, but they seldom talk about the flip side which is losing.

Losing in the trap means getting robbed, getting shot, catching a case, going to the joint or going to the grave. You are not an animal even though they think you are. Get loose from the trap! The white powered people want young black men to keep trapping, robbing and killing so they can keep putting them in prison making billions off of them.

While the men are doing time in prisons the black woman has no choice but to become the head of the household, raise fatherless children or become an economical trick for the white man's system.

The government makes about twenty thousand dollars a year per person in prison. They're a few million people in prisons across America which equals billions of dollars spent every day. Young men have to start changing their actions, their wardrobes, their characters and their language.

Speaking of language, what made it cool to call another man a bitch in general conversation? I remember when getting called a bitch by another man was grounds for a fist fight with the possibility of death. Getting called a bitch is like a white man calling a black man a nigger. This is how too many of our young men talk to each other which is messed up. To accept being called a bitch especially by another man kills your self-worth and dishonors your manhood whether you believe it or not.

Some men think that they're women so they may be bitches but not this one. If you're cool with being called a bitch, you may need to look up the definition and find another pet name for yourself. More power to you my brother but if you were to ever call me one you might end up getting hit in the mouth.

Young men, it's time to change.

In the book of Ecclesiastes, you will read that there's a time and season for everything. There's a time to be a thug, there's a time hustle, there's a time to chill, and there's a time to show your muscle. There's a time for everything you feel you have to do. I know how you feel when you have to get it like you live. I've been there done that. I have a 25-year career criminal history. I sold drugs for 20 years, and they have destroyed half of my life. I have some really bad memories.

The Criminal Justice system has made thousands off of me from arrests, medical and ambulance bills, lawyers, extortion from the police department, probation, work release, commissary, phone calls, house arrest and far as my social security is concerned, they owe me 100s of thousands of dollars.

I know about God's law, commercial law and some of the legislation of the Moors, so I know what's up. I've been to prison three times, and I have a whole lot of arrests, so I know how a lot of my young thugs feel. We being products of the environment have seemed to have forgotten that we being black people have been through too much to not want to change and overcome these criminal roadblocks. We should have a burning desire to get free from the trap.

You can keep the trap attitude but the motive, purpose, and location must change. It's time to turn the school into the trap and grind getting those grades and try to make it to college. It's time to turn a job into the trap and grind getting those work hours and grind even harder to get a promotion. It's time to turn a good church, or mosque into the trap and grind learning some good virtues. It's time to change the trapping utensils into pens, pencils, paper, blueprints, education apps, books and book bags.

The whole goal of the street hustler's life should be creating wealth to become 100% legit. Young men if you are deeply involved in illegal activities try your best to change your game and become 100% legit! Easy E went legit! This attitude will change the possibility of a felony conviction, a prison sentence or an early death will no longer keep you stuck in poverty, uneducated, with no hope for your future.

Change! Stop playing craps with your life and throwing rocks at the penitentiary. Easy money isn't the safest money! Take your ass back to school! Open up some type of business. This will occupy your time and keep your mind off of crime. Get the message; it's time to start something new.

The Originators

I have repeatedly talked about white power throughout this book as being a powerful and dark negative force. For years, this dominating power that proceeds out of the European race has totally manipulated the minds of many. People seem to forget that Kings, Queens, language, religion, mathematics all have originated from the African race. I believe this would be Black Power! The black, brown, red, yellow, gold or tannish colored people were the first here and the first in control.   Then came white power and American white power, white Christianity and white slaves masters. White power made torture and slavery legal.

The previous white slave masters used the Bible verses in Ephesians 6:5, 1Peter 2:18 and Colossians 3:22 to justify slavery amongst the African, Asian and Indian human beings. This brainwashing tactic distorted the goodness that's in Christianity by creating a way for slaves and slave masters to worship the same white God.

The slave masters never taught slaves about their ancestors who formed the first one God religion. It was thousands of years before Judaism, Islam, and Christianity. The name of this god was the sun disc god Aten and the religion was founded by the African Pharaoh king Amen-Hotep. He changed his name to Akhenaten to support the good will of Aten. His prominent African wife was named Queen Nefertiti, and she is still being held in high esteem today. This is Black Power. Where were white kings and queens way back then? Answer: There were none!

The first biblical hue-man kingdom belonged to Adam and Eve. Adam was a reddish brown color, and the Nile River flowed through the Garden of Eden where they were at. This river began in Africa and broke into four rivers and the first river was called Pishon. This river flowed through a land that the Bible speaks about the first precious metal and the first precious gemstones. The yellow metal was gold, and the stone was onyx, the black stone. This is Biblical evidence of Black Power!

Moving to the Noah era, in Genesis, you will find that Noah had three sons that were three different colors. The first son Shem was red, the second son Ham was black, and the third son Japheth was pale or white. Ham and his descendants were cursed to be slaves forever to his red and white brothers. There have been times in history where all races have been slaves but the black race I believe have gone through the same persecutions as the children of Israel and Jesus Christ. They were the first race to own and dominate everything so therefore they were the first to be tempted by the devil.

The former slave masters failed to keep reading to the slaves about the descendants of Ham, who were Kings. The sons of Ham were Nimrod, Egypt, Cush, Ethiopia, and Canaan. So any name that has Ham, Sheba, Egypt or Cush has some form of black, brown, red, tan or yellow in their DNA make up. The white man has forced billions to believe the characters in the Bible are white, even though most of the Hero's in the Bible were African or Asiatic.

White Christian America does not support these black biblical truths because 95% of all Bibles and movies show images are European Egyptians and European patriarchs. Do you know that the most famous people in the Bible either have lived in Africa, made a baby with an African or visited Africa? Do you know that your Bible says God called Jesus out of Africa and not Europe? Africa is the Motherland. Africa was chosen. Africa is Black Power! All of Africa, North, South, East, and West Africa. All of the indigenous tribes of Africa share African bloodlines that were separate from the white man.

In fact, all of the Hero's in the Bible are descendants of ancestors with African and Asian bloodlines.

From Adam to Jesus there are biblical facts that confirm that the African and Asian race are the Originators of earth. We had the power! We had all of the wealth. We had the riches, precious metals and stones. We ruled the world but then we were tempted by the white devil and pride entered in and we were judged.

Then white power took over. The worldly power that was once black power, was transferred to the Caucasians when they migrated from Africa and Asia, to Europe and the Caucus mountains. When they were in the Caucus Mountains, I believe there were some experiments and deals with Satan against the African and Asian nations. The white man's world began to take form.

Black Kings and Queens of Africa were stripped of their crowns and transformed into slaves, due to the invasion of the racist white man and the white man's religion. The invasion on one of the oldest religions was a black and white situation. This Asian religion was Hinduism, and lighter skin Aryans stole the darker skin Aryans cross.

Now the Aryans are European white racists. It's the same racist invasion that took place against the Mali Empire of Timbuktu, in Africa. It was the empire of Islam, and it was governed by the wealthiest King of the African world, Mansa Moussa. This man is rumored to have had more money than the Roths and the Rocks. The only difference is he gave so much money away in gold to poor people, that he depreciated the gold value for seven years.

The invasion of Africa transformed South Africa into European white Africa. The invasion of America turned Indians and Africans into European cloned Americans. This same invasion is still going on today against all the continents that start with A and end with A, from the one continent that starts with E and ends with E.

The letter E describes their purpose and it secretly lets you know that 1 race the Europeans, from the one continent Europe, wants to rule Everything on the Earth, and they are the E Pluribus Unum. But you know what though?

The oppression from the whites,
everybody knows all it wasn't right. Nothing
will never change unless you're willing to
fight. I'm not lying my people have lived and
died, not knowing who they are because they
believe in white lies. Somebody tell me how
much does freedom cost? The cross, white
Jesus, 1776, 1863, 1865, 1964, 2008-16 we
still out here lost. It's time to wake up and

*find out the truth, unite with the thirst of
knowledge and create a better me and a
better you.*

*Remember we are here now and we are the
Originators.*

---

1 Nation

I was desperately searching for information about how to globally change the black nation as a whole and came across some enlightening information from the Late Malcolm X. He started an organization called the OAAU, Organization of Afro-American Unity. This organization had incredible core values and planned to bring the African American men and women together, to build an economic infrastructure of power, love, land and sovereignty.

This organization came from the OAU, Organization of African Unity and later became the AU, African Union. One Nation of African Americans would be beautiful if black Americans would participate. The vision of a real United States of Africa and the African-Asiatic Union. The problem with the unification is black people stay divided in America.

The Nation of Islam, who people always talk bad about, stands united in America. They define black power and their seed the final call allows you to see all the corruption and racism in America. There is a serious misunderstanding between black Americans and their religions. If we continue to stay confused, we will continue to remain divided.

The white racists are devil worshipers and Christians. They are separate but equal because they work together and help each other because they're white.

This is why they seem to always win. We are Christians, Muslims or in other religions, and we argue, disagree and kill each other because we have allowed the white devil to brainwash us into believing that we are unequal. Like my righteous and loving Most High God is better than your righteous and loving Most High God and you're going to hell if you don't worship my God. Truth, Peace, and Love is God. Our Father, Our Mother. Anything that does not possess these three attributes is not of God. We have become blind to this fact choosing to hold on to doctrines and laws taught by the white man that keep black people separated. Therefore, we fight each other and seem to always lose. If we would one day come together, we would win. I think people don't know what religions are. Religions are gangs that do different rituals, and they have different literature, laws and belief systems. Whatever religion connects you to the truth and the light, is the religion for you.

If black people in various faiths, positions, and social standings could one day except peace between each other and understand what separate but equal means, the disrespect to religions and each other will disappear. After peace, love and respect for each other and each other's religion finally happens, this is where there needs to be a new alliance, a black coalition, an entirely new government.

A state of black individuals creating a strong force of power, the real power, Black Power! A table of contents resembling one like the seven principles of Kwanzaa should be taught and followed. The organizations the OAAU, AU, FAU, have core values that are similar to principles of Kwanzaa. They describe the proper, social, spiritual and economical design. Universal peace and love will bring a new attitude and character for all black Americans. There should be an alliance between all African American religions and organizations. Then there should be reformation marches, boycotts, holiday boycotts and speeches.

The first reformation event should be the boycott of July 4th. This boycott would force a revolutionary change. This holiday has made billions over the years from black Americans from food, fireworks and alcohol sales. Black America has been celebrating this holiday in vain because in July 1776, in no way was anyone that was black all the way free.

Black Americans were still getting raped, tortured and murdered in 1776. A black person wasn't even an American back then, but yet we still continue to lie to our children and tell them that we as America became free on this day. No! White America became free; we black folks were slaves on this day. The truth is the truth, and a lie is a lie!

If you subtract the Emancipation Proclamation of September 22nd, 1862 and black America was still slaves, from the Civil Rights Act of 1964, that's 102 years of oppression on paper! Now subtract the Declaration of Independence of 1776, when lawmakers still owned slaves, from the Civil Rights Act of 1964, that's a total of 188 years of oppression on American paper!!!!

There has never been generational gifts of 40 acres and a mule, nor a stimulus bill or a bailout bill to end impoverished African Americans. I think there's a whole lot of money that's owed to black Africa America. Since we are indigenous people with historical ties to the continent that had all the gold and diamonds, I think we need like between 1 billion to 100 billion a state. 100

billion a state, 50 states is 5 trillion. This money would create the financial strength that is needed to help rebuild our communities across Africa America and different regions around the world. These funds would buy land for farming, schools, hospitals, industrialization, real estate, security services and assist with feeding the hungry, giving housing to the homeless, creating businesses, jobs and vocational training for children, adults and ex-cons.

Three of the leading careers for this Movement would be coordinators, teachers, and counselors. They would work together to counsel youth and teach children trades early in life, providing summer job projects and nonviolent entertainment. All religions that practice peace and love and forgiveness should unite for as one black race for this Movement. Those who do not practice these virtues should not be allowed in this Movement. There should be respect and no disrespect to each other's religion.

We could make some changes that could positively affect each and every black American in America. The only other way to create an economical change is for 20 million black Americans invest 1 dollar a day, for one year, under one account.

This project would generate billions in interest and multiply the 365 dollar investment. A movement of economic unity would change the economy.

Did you not know that black folk run the entire economy? We make the less and buy the most. This is the monopoly of white power to keep black folk as the help and white folk as the helper.

We are the labor, the major consumers, and the spenders. We get our money from the white man and give it all back to him. We spend over a trillion a year.

What do you think will happen if the entire black American population would boycott all holidays and all spending in all white stores? I believe eyes would open.

This event would be the real Black Friday. Black Monday, Tuesday, Wednesday and Thursday, the Blackout. We can build and fund our corporations and communities with our monies and skills. They didn't want blacks in their establishments so stop forcing your way in theirs. Keep our money power in the black community. We can make the new Black Wall Street.

If we all came together as one, economic mountains would move. If we don't come together, they will continue to be in the way. We need to unite as one black nation, under God, indivisible with liberty and justice for all.

- ➤ Will there ever be a day that we can move to higher heights of peace and love?
- ➤ Can we learn how to treat one another with the full totality of respect due, one human to another?
- ➤ Can we quit misjudging each other because of the way someone looks?
- ➤ Can we unite without an evil motive? Can we treat each other how we want to be treated?

Only if you believe.

African American Flag

Red represents the blood that was shed from millions of black men, women and children. Black represents the black soil of the ground and the color of the people. Green represents the color of vegetation, fertility and the land of Africa. Pan African, Afro-American and Black Liberation. These are some of the titles of the red, black and green flag that was established in 1920, after a racist song depicting that every race has a flag except the coon.

The UNIA, Universal Negro Improvement Association and the ACL, African Communities League, declared the rights as an African American and adopted the African flag. The significance and right as an African American was quoted by Marcus Garvey, setting the grounds for African Americans possessing a flag of their own. This flag is thetrue flag for African Americans. The American flag and the Confederate flag have <u>nothing</u> to do with black people. They are flags that were created by white people for white people.

You may say America is your country, and the American flag is your flag but if you're black you're truthfully lying to yourself. Is the color black in either of the two white American flags? No! The color white is not in any of the African American flags because white people have <u>nothing</u> to do with it. They will never know the struggle. Many European Americans will not acknowledge the red, black and green flag.

They are separate and don't let the current integration fool you into thinking everything has changed, and everybody is equal. They still look at us as unequal; they still hate us, and they're still murdering us, so they are still the adversary.

Every time you hold the American flag up high, you honor a country who is responsible for the deaths of some of your deceased ancestors.

In the 18 and 1900's, the white man brainwashed black Americans into believing that the American flag represents freedom, bravery and justice. During this brainwashing process, black folk was going through slavery, forced to be cowards and dealing with every aspect of injustice. The red, black and green flag is something that we can say was created for us by us! Our forefathers and ancestors were martyred to establish the integrity and honor of being proud to be a black person. Our blood, our skin, our land. The African American flag is the banner of Africa right here in America. Black Pride! Black Power! Black Nation stand up!

Your Life Matters

What is your mission in life? Why were you born in this destructive world that has become a wild jungle? In the jungle are many creatures and the snakes are the wisest and sneakiest. The snakes are everywhere you go in the world, and some of these may be your family members, so beware.

The world is violent, and there is so much killing that it appears nobody cares about life anymore. Life is a job and an occupation in itself. It's also a constant tug of war between good and evil. A war against one's thoughts of self-worth and a war against those that you associate with every day.

One of the main lessons in life is to know how to control yourself. You have internal control and external control. Your internal control is the source of your consciousness. Your decisions control your mouth and your body. For every action, there is a reaction. When you consciously make bad decisions, the outcome can lead to the two types of possible deaths. Prison or the grave.

Your external control is your family, peers and communication devices. External programming has the power to influence your internal control and may lead you to become out of control. When this happens, you have to get back in control or risk being trapped in an uncontrollable state. It's easy to get comfortable in this state of mind even when it's out of control, due to fear of what life might be in a controlled state. Those who refuse to break this cycle will remain uncontrollable. This state of mind causes serious problems, and one stays confused, even when things may seem to be going great.

It's time to take back control of your life and live. Life is for the living, so try to live well. The more you strive to live a better life; the more tests, trials, and tribulations will come your way. Although things may seem not to be going your way, God will see you through it. God is the greatest teacher, and He controls time. No man can defeat time.

Time changes everything. The way things look, the way people look, the way people talk and walk, the way people dress, the way people act, the things people do, the places people go, the places people live, the way people feel, our lives are changed by the hands of time.

So if you see or know someone who thinks he is the strongest, wealthiest, most powerful person on earth, they are headed to the same place you're going. To the grave! So while you're still here, it's best to live the best life that you can live.

To know how to live, you have to seek knowledge. You must seek wisdom relentlessly and force yourself to train, study and exercise your mind, body and spirit. Find out everything about everything. Be optimistic through the dark times. There are so many topics to learn. Have faith in yourself. You can do it and know that you can, there's nothing to it. It's in you and you hold the master plan to your life.

Have faith in a good natured higher power that will make your life complete and bring you peace. Dedicate yourself, discipline yourself and focus on what's real. Keep your spiritual weapons of war close and meditate on them.

Try to limit yourself from impurities such as drugs, immoral sex, alcohol, cigarettes, etc. Find your unique talent and condition it. Love yourself and try to stay in a positive state of mind even under harsh circumstances.

Study these things and stay active and in time, things will change in your life. Your life matters in the hands of time. I hope you enjoyed this book. There is a beginning, and there's an end, all good things come to an end, and this is the end.

David Lee the Author

Wonder how things would have been if everything was the other way around

---

Skits
Trading Places

The story begins with an 116-year-old white historian telling his story on how far the white race has come. His name is Christopher Columbus Muhammed and now let's begin:

It's now 2008 and were in the first term of the first American white president. All of the others before him were black and held their offices in the black house.

"I'm so glad we finally have a white president." "Thank You Jesus!" "I mean we came a long way white people." "I remember back in the segregated days it was black only everything."
"It was black only schools, black only churches, black only restaurants and restrooms, and they were those harsh Jerome Crow black laws." "While all this was going on the racist apartheid was going on in South Europe."
"The laws are still so hard for us white folk; we are always being pulled over by black police, and police brutality is at an ultimate high." "There has recently been 66 unarmed white men that have been murdered by black policemen across the nation." "I haven't seen these type actions from the police since the civil rights movement."
"I remember some of the police were members of the notorious group the KKKK [Klu Klux Klan Killers]."
"They wore black hoods and robes posing as dead Confederate soldiers, and they used to scream Black power! Black Power!"
"Those black devils used to say they were Christians, but to me, it seemed like they were devils with the types of things they were doing." "They were responsible for some the deaths of my white brothers and sisters." "They would hang white people, rape white people, burn our houses and would kill some of their people if they found out they were helping us whites."
"I can even take you back further to the beginning, way before white history month, and that fake Declaration of Independence." "I call it fake because whites were still slaves in 1776."

"Listen, now before America became America there was a meeting." "This meeting was around the 1500's, and it was between 2 royal tribes." "The tribes were the Zulu Africans and the Cherokee Indians." "They came up with an exploration business plan, and they called it The Land and Sea Frontier."
"This project consisted of 2000 ships that would take voyages sailing through the Atlantic Ocean to seek out new lands and new civilizations." "The Royals would then confiscate land, people, and resources." "They called these voyages treks, something like Star Trek but this was not the trek of space, this was the trek of land and water."
"The ships sailed to Europe and America and the Royals decreed Terms, Acts, and Treaties to the people. The Royals colonized the land and traded with the Europeans." "A war eventually broke out, and the Europeans were defeated." "The chiefs of the Dutch, French, Spanish, and the most powerful the British, were no match for the military power and weapons of the royal African and Indian tribes."
"Millions of Europeans became slaves, and they were taken to Africa, Asia, and Australia to endure hard labor persecutions and oppression." "The New World America was the land that first belonged to us whites and those racist red, brown, and black devils made us slaves to our own land."
"The white slaves were often called names like honky, homo, faggot, red neck, pig, peckerwood, cracker, cunt, white boy, white beach and white trash." "The slaves had to work long hours in the sun picking cotton, marijuana, tobacco and beans. Their skin would peel and burn, and many died from sunburn and heat

exhaustion." "Slaves were always whipped, and many women and children were raped."

"The slaves were forced to grow their blond hair long, change their names to African, Asian, and Indian names, and they were compelled to take African Christianity, Hinduism, and Islam as a religion."

"The great European-American writer Allah Hailey even made a movie about these slavery times called STOOR."

"In this movie the most shocking part was when the white slave named Tommy, was tied up and whipped by black slave masters until he said his name was Coonta. It was such a terrible time for the white man back then, and if it had not been for the Lord and blacks that supported us, the laws probably never would have changed, and we would never have become free or somewhat free."

"That was then, and this is now, and we're somewhat integrated I guess." "The racial discrimination that we suffered in the past is still living today." "I'm still glad we got a white president, though, at least I'm alive to see that, even though I know the black devils got something terrible up their sleeves. THE END."

The American Party

This skit represents the continuing drama that is upholding the government across America. The government officials are called the *Actors,* and the American citizens are known as the *Audience.* The movie script and the laws are called Bills, Treaties, Acts and of course the Party. I am the director. *"Now is everybody ready to begin?" "Props everyone, now*

Action!!!!" The *Actors* enter this large beautiful white building with oval rooms and offices. Accompanying them is a former president, a Catholic bishop, colonists, councilmen, a treasurer and members of the Congress. They were dressed in black suits, and they're trying to get their proposal together. They are adding things in the script and taking things out. *Actor 1 "Don't wanna give up to much information, we wanna surprise the Audience." "This is going to be such a great Party." "Is everybody ready?" "Ok now invite the Audience in."* *Actor 2 "Oh wait a minute!", "call in the authorities first; they have the party favors."* In comes the military with their guns and medals of Honor. They bring with them food, alcohol, tobacco, drugs and Bibles. *Military soldiers 1 "They will believe us if they are full, high and intoxicated with Jesus." "Amen" Bishop "Amen." "Ok now places everyone." "Invite the Audience in."* The authorities open the 20-foot doors of the beautiful white building and in walks the leaders and representatives of all 50 states. There are different nationalities but mainly just 3.

The 1st group attending the party were the white southern Europeans. They came in the party smiling because some of the Actors are their family, friends and business partners. Whatever the Actors have planned won't affect them because they're in on all deals. Oh, I forgot to tell you, this party costs big time. They have their nice chariots outside; they brought in their wives, and they have on white suits and white hats. Some were wearing white hoods and white robes.

The 2nd group attending the party were the poor Europeans; they came in half smiling. They weren't all dressy like the first group, and some of them wouldn't even talk to them. The southerners didn't like the poor Europeans because they supported the 3rd group.

The 3rd group attending the party were the African Americans and half of them didn't come because the first group told them they were still slaves. They came in the party half smiling, some frowning, some were dressed up, some still had their civil war uniform on, some were still hurting, and some wanted to kill something.

Finally, the 4th group attending the party were the Indians; they were late because they had to walk 500 miles to get to the party. The warrior tribe was not allowed in and the other more calm Indians didn't want to come in either until they found out that tobacco and alcohol was inside. Their spears and axes were confiscated and they were allowed in. They were shirtless and had on war paint. None of the Indians were smiling. *Actor 1 "All the guests are present sir,"* *Bishop "Let us eat and drink"* He then says a couple Hail Mary's and everybody begins to eat and drink. Some Africans, Europeans, and Indians are just staring at each other knowing that this party is very strange. A few Indians and Africans are not participating at all in the festivities; they really want to kill all the racist Europeans in the place, even the non-racist poor ones. So a few hours pass and people are socializing, smoking, and just chilling.

Actor 2 "Attention everyone, attention everyone, we are about to reveal unto you the reason for this wonderful party," "bring out the treaty!!!!" One of the Actors brings the treaty to the former president, and he begins to read. After 2 minutes into the reading of the treaty all of the talking and smiles stop, and there was total silence, until the crashing noise of glass shattering from a spear coming through the window, striking the former president in the heart. The soldiers scoop up the former president's body and throw him to the side; they then shoot all of the Indians outside along with the suspect. Women are crying, and everybody is upset not because of all the commotion, but because of what the treaty stated.

It stated that: *All of the land is ours the Actors. All of the laws we pass must be obeyed even if they're wrong. You must work and pay taxes to us until you die. We will take a percentage of your wages and everything you buy until you die. We will enforce the same laws and deduct the same taxes from your children after you die. We can remove our support from you anytime we feel, for no reason. We will no longer accept your gold, silver, livestock, or other commodities for purchasing our products. You must buy and sell with our paper money system that will put us the Actors in power and you the Audience in debt, but we don't care, we will just make more money until the economy forces A New World Order. This is just the beginning of the Treaty. Members of the Congress "If you the leaders of the states do not sign this treaty at this Party tonight, you will be shot and your women will become our baby mammas."* So the leaders of the Audience signed the treaty and everybody begins to leave, then one the members of the treasury says *"Wait I forgot to give you guys the BILL!"* He then charges the American audience 666 million dollars for the beautiful white building and all of the party favors. *"Don't worry"* he says *"you have plenty of time to pay the bill off."* So the Audience leaves the beautiful white building and the Actors high five each other and have a toast to the good life. They then take their wives on vacations and their mistresses on shopping sprees. The end.

Works Cited

Cappannelli S. C. & Cappannelli G. (2002). Say Yes to Change: 25 Keys To Winning in Times of Transition. Better Way Books.

Cohen J. & Solomon N. (2002). Adventures in Media Land Behind the News Beyond the Pundits. Common Courage Press.

Dee K. M. (1987). Wild Wild West [Recorded by K. M. Dee]. On How Ya Like Me Now. New York New York USA: Jive Records.

en.wikipedia.org/wiki/Pledge_of_Allegiance. (n.d.). Pledge of Allegiance. Wikipedia.

Holy Bible. (1988 8990 9193 96 2004). Holy Bible King James Version Life Application Study Bible. Wheaton IL: Tyndale House.

Holy Bible. (1995 96 98). New International Readers Version (NIRV Edition). Colorado Springs CO: Biblica Inc.

The Qur'an Third U.S. Edition (2009) Translated by Abdullah Yusuf Ali Tahrike Tarsile Qur'an Inc. New York

Prophet Clare Elizabeth (2000) Fallen Angels Origins of Evil: Why Church Fathers Suppressed the Book of Enoch, and It's Starting Revelations

Icke D. (1999). The Biggest Secret. APS Sales and Fulfillment.

Lawson G. & William O. (2007). The Brotherhoods: The True Story of Two Cops who Murdered for the Mafia. Pocketbooks.

Shale P. (1987). Warrior Within: A Guide to Inner Power. Delta Group Press.

Duiker J. William& Spielvogel J. Jackson Pennsylvania State University (1998) World History 2nd Edition

Wadsworth Publishing Company International Thomson Publishing Inc.

Smith P. (1990). Trial by Fire: A Peoples History of the Civil War and Reconstruction Period (Peoples History of USA). Penguin Books.

Wikipedia. (n.d.). http://commonsenseconspiracy.com/2012/10/lyndon-johnson-the-n-word-and-the-concept-of-the-democrat-plantation/. Wikipedia.

Scott Jill (2015) Fools Gold (Recorded by Jill Scott) Atlantic Records 15th anniversary of her debut album who is Jill Scott? Words and Sounds Vol. 1

Baum L Frank W. W. Denslow (1900) The Wonderful Wizard of Oz George M. Hill Company

Metro-Goldwyn-Mayer (1939 film) The Wizard of OZ

Columbia Universal Motown (1978 film) The Wiz

CBS -MGM (1956 TV) The Wizard of Oz

Wonder Stevie (1966) Some Day At Christmas Tamla Records

The Emotions (1973) What do the Lonely Do at Christmas Stax Records

Vandross Luther (1976) At Christmas Time Atlantic Records

Young Andrew (1998) An Easy Burden: The Civil Rights Movement and the Transformation of America Baylor University Press

Cohen Jeff (1993) Adventures in Medialand: Behind the News Beyond the Pundits Common Courage Press

Ferrel-Mendez Ana (2011) The Dark Secrets of the GAOTU: Shattering the Deception of Free Masonry Destiny Image Publishers

Lee Spike 40 Acres and A Mule Filmworks (1988) School Daze musical drama Columbia Pictures

Cosby Bill & Poussaint F. Alvin M.D. (2007) Come On
People: On the Path from Victims to Victors Thomas
Nelson Inc.

Priest Dana & Arkin William (2011) Top Secret America:
The Rise of The New American Security State Little
Brown and Company

Sadler Robert with Marie Chapin: (1975) (2012) The
Emancipation of Robert Sadler The Powerful Story of A
Twentieth-Century Plantation Slave Bethany House

Lelyveld Joseph Pulitzer Prize winner (1986) Move Your
Shadow: South Africa Black and White Penguin Books

Pledge of Allegiance and its "under God"
phrase. (n.d.). Retrieved from
http://www.religioustolerance.org/nat_pled1.htm

The number of the Beast: 666- The Forbidden
Knowledge www.theforbiddenknowledge.com>words

Dedication

I dedicate this book to the greatest musician who touched my world. My Mother an Indianapolis Indiana gospel legend, Ms. Alice Hopkins.

I would like to thank Paulette Hayden, my confidant, editor and great debater for all of your help and support over this 18-month progress of creating a substance filled book.

I love you, Dorian David Lee, thank you for understanding my commitment and dedication to write this book to help heal the world.

To my brother and sisters Keith Hopkins, Monique Lee and Aleta Hopkins thanks for all your love and support through the good and bad times.

To the Indiana Department of Corrections, for sitting me down giving me the opportunity to read all of the great books that helped open my mind to the inconsistencies of this world I thank you.

To my readers and supporters, I hope you enjoyed The Black Truth behind White Lies and stay tuned for my next venture.

God Bless.

David Lee the Author